Cabin Boy to Advent Crusader

by
Virgil Robinson

Illustrated by
Harry Baerg

TEACH Services, Inc.
P U B L I S H I N G
www.TEACHServices.com

I0154024

World rights reserved. This book or any portion thereof may not be copied or reproduced in any form or manner whatever, except as provided by law, without the written permission of the publisher, except by a reviewer who may quote brief passages in a review.

This book was written to provide truthful information in regard to the subject matter covered. The author assumes full responsibility for the accuracy of all facts and quotations as cited in this book. The opinions expressed in this book are the author's personal views and interpretation of the Bible, Spirit of Prophecy, and/or contemporary authors and do not necessarily reflect those of TEACH Services, Inc.

This book is sold with the understanding that the publisher is not engaged in giving spiritual, legal, medical, or other professional advice. If authoritative advice is needed, the reader should seek the counsel of a competent professional.

Copyright © 2005, 2012 TEACH Services, Inc.
ISBN-13: 978-1-57258-312-2 (Paperback)
ISBN-13: 978-1-57258-829-5 (ePub)
ISBN-13: 978-1-57258-830-1 (Kindle/Mobi)
Library of Congress Control Number: 2005921831

Published by
TEACH Services, Inc.
P U B L I S H I N G
www.TEACHServices.com

Preface

WHEN in the years 1845 and 1846 a little company of Christians stepped out from the ranks of thousands of Adventists and began to keep the seventh-day Sabbath, there were three who had taken part in proclaiming the first and second angels' messages who now became prominent in heralding the third angel's message. These were James White, Ellen Harmon, and Joseph Bates. Pioneers of the pioneers, they must ever be regarded as among the earliest workers in the history of the Seventh-day Adventist Church.

Of the two characteristics of the remnant church as prophesied in Revelation 12:17, one was to be the *testimony of Jesus*, which is the *Spirit of prophecy*. This gift of God was manifested through the messages borne by Ellen Harmon, who became Ellen G. White after her marriage to James White. The second characteristic was the keeping of the commandments of God. The one commandment which virtually the whole world was ignoring at that time was the fourth. It was to the task of proclaiming, exalting, and championing the binding obligations of the seventh-day Sabbath that Joseph Bates devoted the last twenty-five years of his life.

A fairly complete biography covering the life and work of James and Ellen White may be found in the book *Life Sketches*. There is no similar current work dealing with the life and labors of Joseph Bates.

No history of the rise and development of the remnant church during its formative years could claim to be either accurate or complete if it failed to make frequent mention of Joseph Bates and to emphasize the important part he played.

It should be remembered that he was not a young man when he began to proclaim the Sabbath truth. Whereas Ellen was only eighteen and James White twenty-six when they were married and began to keep the Sabbath, Joseph Bates was fifty-four in that same year. He had been a preacher of the first angel's message for years before the great disappointment in 1844. One might expect that with this experience and background he would step forward to occupy the position of leader in the infant movement. Joseph Bates was not that kind of man. Never seeking the limelight, he was perfectly satisfied to do his duty as he saw it, trusting the Lord from day to day to reveal to him his particular work and then give him strength to accomplish it.

To his many friends during those early days he was known as much by the title Captain Bates as Elder Bates. To understand the reason for this, one must examine the story of his early life. His autobiography entitled *The Life of Joseph Bates* was published in Battle Creek, Michigan, more than ninety years ago. A few copies of this rare book are still in existence. In this book he traces the story of his twenty-one years spent sailing the seas, his conversion, his advance in health reform, and how, in the end, he became the great Sabbath champion of the movement.

In these days when the feeble resources of the pioneers—what they achieved with them still amazes us today—have been multiplied a thousandfold, it is hoped that this story may inspire the remnant people of God anew, leading them to throw into the task which still faces them the same ardor and devotion, the same sacrificial service and fearless courage, that marked the life of Joseph Bates.

Table Contents

About fifty feet above the deck Joseph misjudged the distance to the next spar and fell backward off the mast.

Chapter One

The Call of the Sea

TWO fair-haired boys sat swinging their bare legs over the edge of the pier fronting the harbor of New Bedford, Massachusetts, their eyes as blue as the arching sky overhead or the sea which stretched to the far-distant horizon. School was out for the day, and there was an hour of free time. The breeze blew in softly from the sea. Gulls screamed as they swooped for tasty morsels of food on the surface of the bay. Tied up to another pier not far away was a trim three-masted schooner unloading barrels of raw sugar from the French West Indies. The bright flag fluttering from its mast, with its sixteen stars and many stripes, proclaimed that it was an American ship. The boys looked idly down at the water many feet below them as it swirled past the stout posts supporting the pier. The year was 1803, and their country was only twenty-seven years old.

"Look at how fast the tide is coming in," remarked Philip Smith to his younger companion. I think that French ship over there is going to sail as soon as it turns," he continued.

"Yes," replied Joseph Bates, his eleven-year-old friend. "Every day I keep wondering when Captain Howland and his ship, the *Firefly* will arrive from West Africa. I have not forgotten his promise to get me two coconuts when he makes his next trip to the Gold Coast. I want to be here when he returns."

The boys talked on of their hopes and plans for the future. Joseph had already decided that he wanted to be a sailor. Day after day he had come down to the wharves and talked with the sailors as they returned from long voyages to Europe, Africa, South America, or the West Indies.

The lowering sun warned them that they should hasten home to do the chores which fell to the lot of all boys in those early days. Joseph made his way up the street to the comfortable house where he lived with his parents and his brothers and sisters. His good mother welcomed him with a smile, and he hastened to perform his usual duties. At the sound of footsteps on the walk the children went forth to welcome their father, whose return marked the high point of the day. The family gathered around the kitchen table to enjoy together the evening meal. Mother had a good meal for them that night with plenty of home-baked whole-wheat bread and freshly churned butter. The dishes washed and put away, the father conducted evening worship.

"Tell us a story, Father," came from the little ones as they made a circle around his chair in the cheerful kitchen.

Mother Bates smiled as she brought forth her spinning wheel and began her work.

"What shall I tell you about tonight?" he asked with a smile.

"All about the war, Father. Tell us about the time when you were with General Washington and what you did in Valley Forge."

The children had reason to be proud of their father's war record. Had he not been among the first to leave the little town of Wareham, not far from Plymouth, when the first call for minutemen came in that fateful summer of 1776? Through seven long years he had remained with the Continental Army, serving his country loyally through good times and bad, through victories and defeats. When peace was made, he had returned to his home town to be married and then had moved to Rochester, where Joseph was born. No wonder Joseph and his brothers and sisters always thrilled to hear their father tell of his exploits in the war which had won their country's independence.

Had young Joseph decided to become a soldier like his father, no one would have been surprised. But growing up in New Bedford, a seaport town to which the family moved when he was only a year old, he had grown healthy and strong on the fresh sea air which blew so steadily from far out over the Atlantic. The lad never tired of watching that sea when it was calm and the waves washed softly on the shore; but equally fascinating to him were the winter months when winds lashed it into fury and the waves rolled in wild and strong.

Joseph knew how cruel that sea could be. There was not a year when some fishing boat did not sail away, never to return. As he stood on the wharf when the fishing fleet sailed each spring for the Grand Banks of Newfoundland, he knew that the question in every heart was, Which boat will not return this year? Whose children will be orphans and their wives widows ere winter come again? Yet, in spite of this, his love for the sea grew stronger year by year.

Many times he spoke of his secret longings to his mother, begging her to give her consent and to speak for him to his father, of whom he was not a little afraid, for permission to go to sea. For a long time his father, a prosperous businessman, refused to discuss the matter. It was his hope that Joseph would come into the office with him. Joseph was willing to wait, and while waiting, he dreamed.

As Joseph neared the age of fifteen, his parents realized that some decision had to be made, so they talked the matter over together.

"Why not let him take a short voyage to some coastal point, perhaps to Boston?" suggested his father. "Who knows? It might give him such a dose of seasickness that he would never want to see the sea again."

So it was decided that the next time Joseph's uncle made a trip to Boston in the small coastal vessel he owned, the lad would go with him.

Hopefully the parents greeted their son as the ship glided into the bay to tie up again in New Bedford harbor. One look at his beaming face told them that there had been no change in Joseph's attitude toward a sailor's life.

"Do you think you still want to be a sailor?" the father asked, although he knew all too well what the answer would be.

"Oh, Father," Joseph replied, "this has been the most wonderful thing I have ever done. How soon can I go again? I want to see Europe, Africa, perhaps South America, or even China!"

Deciding that there was nothing to be gained by refusing the lad's desires any further, they began looking for a ship with a captain to whom they might with confidence entrust their son. Lying at that very time in New Bedford was the *Fanny*, a new ship which was due to sail shortly for New York, there to load a cargo for Europe. Father Bates made arrangements for Joseph to go with the ship as a cabin boy. Joseph lacked just one month of being fifteen years old.

11

A few days later Mr. and Mrs. Bates stood on the pier and watched the ship disappearing in the distance. When would they see him again? There was no wireless in those days and no fast mail service across the seas. It would probably be months before they saw him or even heard from him.

The *Fanny* first went westward and made for New York to load a cargo of wheat. On the afternoon it passed along the northern side of Long Island, there was much anxiety as the ship was carefully steered through a very dangerous passage bounded by rocks on both sides. Here the water rushed madly along, and the greatest care had to be taken to prevent the vessel from being dashed to pieces. The pilot stood at the wheel while every man and boy was called on deck and stood ready to change the sails in case of emergency. But the passage was safely negotiated, and two hours later the ship tied up at the pier in the bustling harbor of a growing seaport. Joseph watched with delight as tons of golden wheat poured into the hold. It was a very heavily laden ship which turned her prow toward Europe, so much so that some expressed fears for her safety. But the wind proved mild, and the ship rode all the steadier for her bulky cargo.

One afternoon as the ship was pressing up the English Channel, the lookout noticed a large number of kegs bobbing up and down in the water.

"Something dead ahead!" he sang out with all his might. Sailors pushed to the prow to see what it might be. The sails were shortened to reduce speed, and a small boat was lowered to pick up the barrels. Several of them were brought on deck; they were found to be filled with gin and brandy. When government patrol boats threatened capture, the barrels had been thrown overboard by smugglers, who thus tried to destroy the evidence of their activities.

Arriving at the London docks, the *Fanny* tied up, and English port officials came on board to inspect the cargo. They expressed surprise when they saw how clean and dry the wheat lay under the hatches as they were opened. In a few days the wheat had all been unloaded, and the ship was ready for the return voyage.

The water casks were refilled, water from the Thames River being used for this. Joseph was shocked to see the condition of the water being put into their casks, streaked as it was with green, yellow, and red, mixed with filth from thousands of ships and the scum and wastes of London. After the water had been a few days in the casks, however, the dirt settled to the bottom, and it appeared fresh and clean.

The return voyage was pleasant, but not so speedy as their trip to England. Strong winds from the west were often against them. On a Sunday morning one of the sailors noticed a large shark following the ship. One man brought a large piece of meat, which he fastened to a rope and trailed in the water, hoping that the shark would come near enough to be speared. But the crafty enemy kept out of reach and followed along hour after hour, always on the same side of the ship. Many sailors are very superstitious, believing that when a shark follows a ship, someone is going to die and be buried at sea or someone is going to fall overboard.

That same day toward evening young Joseph was ordered to ascend one of the masts to scan the horizon for any possible vessel. Seeing nothing, he was preparing to descend. When about fifty feet above the deck, he misjudged the distance to the next spar and fell backwards off the mast. When he struck a swinging rope, his fall toward the deck was averted, but he was hurled out into the foaming sea.

After plunging to a considerable depth, Joseph struggled to the surface only to see the vessel rapidly moving away. His heavy clothing, particularly his boots, made swimming almost impossible. The captain and sailors had rushed to the stern. One of the officers caught a glimpse of him and threw a coiled rope with all his might in the direction of the drowning sailor. With his last ounce of strength Joseph reached out, grasped it, and was hauled up on deck, so completely exhausted that he could only lie and gasp.

Suddenly someone remarked, "Where is the shark?" Joseph remembered with a shudder that he had fallen on the very side where the shark had been swimming all day. Not seeing him in his usual place, the men rushed to the other side, where they saw him gliding along quite undisturbed by what was going on. No one knew when he had changed to the other side of the vessel.

As Joseph pondered the events of the day, lying in his hammock that night, he wondered whether the God whom his mother loved and trusted might not have been watching over him. It was very likely, he thought to himself, that at the very moment of his greatest danger she had been praying for him.

Chapter Two

The Shadow of War

DURING the following two years Joseph Bates made a number of voyages to Europe. The month of May, 1809, found him once more in New York City, where he signed on as a deck hand aboard a vessel bound from that port to Archangel, Russia. The sea was full of dangers in those days for both captain and sailors on American ships. A terrible war had been raging in Europe for more than fifteen years. Napoleon, the emperor of the French, had conquered most of the Continent, but he could not get his army to England because of the channel which lay between it and France. In order to weaken the English as much as possible, he commanded that no ship from any country should go into a British port. If one did, then his government would seize it, and the owner would receive nothing. The British government replied by saying that it would seize any ship going to a port in Europe which did not first call at an English port. Thus American ships might be taken by England or France no matter what they did.

The weather was fine for a few days after the ship left port. Then the captain turned the vessel northward, seeking the shortest route to Russia. Soon it became very cold. One morning the sailors were surprised to see a large number of icebergs scattered out over many miles of the sea. Those great masses of ice were slowly heaving up and down, and it took much skill for the sailors to steer the little ship safely through their midst. In the late afternoon they apparently left the bergs behind and came out into the open sea again.

As night came on, a thick fog settled over the sea, blotting out the stars and making it impossible to see more than twenty feet ahead of the ship. As the vessel carried full sail, a strong icy wind drove it forward through the water at great speed. The sailors became alarmed. Suppose they ran into another group of icebergs in the fog? The chief mate spoke to the captain.

"Sir, allow us to haul in the sails and remain here until morning, when perhaps the fog will lift. There is grave danger that we may strike ice."

"No," replied the captain, "we have now left the ice behind us and so have nothing to fear, as the open sea is free. The wind is fine, so there is no reason why we cannot cover many knots tonight."

The mate was not satisfied, but fearing to disobey the captain, he took in none of the sails. He did, however, post a strong lookout. But the thick fog made this of little use. Joseph himself, with a companion, remained on watch until midnight, when they were relieved and went below to sleep. About an hour later they were roused by a frightened cry from the helmsman: "An iceberg! Dead ahead!"

The very next moment there was a dreadful crash. Joseph was pitched out of his bunk and struck his head on the forecastle wall with such force that he lay stunned for a few moments on the floor. Then, struggling to his feet, he found his arms going around the body of his friend and companion Palmer in the inky blackness of the cabin. The other sailors who had been sleeping in the same room had rushed on deck and closed the hatch. Climbing up the ladder, the two who had been left behind tried several times to move the heavy hatch, but in vain. Giving up, they placed their arms around each other's necks and prepared to die. They expected every moment that the ship would sink beneath the waves. They could hear water splashing in through a hole the ice had made somewhere in the side of the vessel. On deck above them all was confusion. They could hear the tramp of many feet mingling with the groans and cries of the sailors begging God to have mercy on them.

Terrible ideas rushed into poor Joseph's mind. "Only sixteen years of life!—here to yield up my account and die and sink with the wrecked ship to the bottom of the ocean, so far from home and friends, without the least preparation or hope of heaven and eternal life."

Suddenly the hatch was lifted, and a voice called out, "Is there anyone below?"

"Yes, let us out!" shouted Palmer. In a few moments he and Joseph were standing on deck beside their mates. They quickly looked over the ship, and in the gloom they could see that her bow lay partly under a shelf of ice, her sails billowing out with the wind which was driving her farther and farther beneath the edge of the iceberg.

Joseph and his friend felt there was little hope of saving the vessel. So they turned their attention to the lifeboat which they hoped to get launched. But they soon saw that even this would not help much, for it was evident that the heavy sea and wind would dash it against the iceberg as soon as it was on the water.

The conscience-stricken captain walked up and said to them in an agitated voice:

"Whatever are you going to do with me, Palmer?"

"I am going to heave you overboard," replied the thoroughly angry sailor.

"There is no use in that," replied the captain. "We shall all of us be in eternity in less than five minutes."

"You should be there sooner than that," replied Palmer. "It is all your fault that we have been wrecked like this."

Joseph Bates seized Palmer by the hand.

"Let him go," he said. "Come with me and let's try the pumps."

Palmer agreed, and to their astonishment they found that the pumps sucked. This fact filled them with new hope. Now the problem was to get the ship free from the iceberg.

"Let go the topgallant sail halyards," called out the chief mate. This was soon done, and the ship now caught the wind from a different angle. Like a lever sliding from under a rock, the ship broke away from the iceberg and in a few minutes was once more riding free in the water. A hasty examination showed that there was much repair work to be done, as one of the masts had been shattered by the collision. Never was dawn more welcome than to Bates and his companions on that vessel. Full sail was once more hoisted, and soon they were scudding along before the gale, bound for Ireland, where they expected to make the necessary repairs on the ship. By working the pumps night and day, they kept her from sinking and safely reached Shannon. Here they were forced to remain for nearly two weeks.

Leaving Ireland, the American ship next fell in with a large convoy of English ships, two or three hundred sail strong, bound for the Baltic and protected by several warships. In order to enjoy this protection, the ship Bates was on traveled with them for a few days. Not far from the coast of Scotland a heavy storm came up. Here they sought to anchor, but during the night a number of the ships broke their cables and were dashed onto the rocky shore. Fortunately the American ship was able to keep ahead of the wind and so escape, leaving the convoy far behind. Now they felt it would be safe to continue their journey around Norway to Archangel.

The sun came up, and all hands rejoiced at their second narrow escape from shipwreck. Their rejoicing was short-lived, however, for they soon saw two strange vessels rapidly overtaking them. As these came nearer, they began firing, and soon cannon balls were splashing into the water around the American ship. In order to save his vessel from serious injury, the captain ordered the sails furled and thus awaited the arrival of the armed ships, which turned out to be Danish privateers. Since Denmark was part of Napoleon's empire at this time, the captain knew he had violated the emperor's law by putting into Shannon, an English port, even if it was only to make repairs on the ship. The larger of the two privateers escorted the American ship to Copenhagen, the capital of Denmark.

As they were nearing the city, the captain, who was part owner of the ship and its cargo, called the crew together and offered to give each sailor a handsome reward when they reached America again if he would testify in court that their boat had come directly from New York and had not stopped at any British port. Joseph Bates refused to agree. This brought upon him some very angry looks from members of the crew, who would lose the promised reward.

A few days later the crew of their ship was taken into a Danish court. Before being asked to testify, Joseph was shown a box about fifteen inches long and eight inches high.

"Do you know what is in that box?" asked the judge.

"No, I do not, sir," replied Joseph.

"It contains a machine with which we cut off the two forefingers and thumb of everyone who swears falsely here. Now hold up the two forefingers and thumb of your right hand and swear to tell the truth."

Joseph did so and carefully related the story of their encounter with the iceberg. He told of how they had taken their ship into the Irish port only to make repairs. They were bound for Russia, one of the countries allied with Napoleon. In spite of this testimony, the judge ruled that by stopping in a British port they had forfeited their ship with all its contents, and they were dismissed from court with nothing at all except the clothing they were wearing that morning.

A few days later some of the American sailors were walking along one of the streets of Copenhagen when they passed the city jail. Here some of the prisoners thrust their hands up to the gratings, showing that they had lost their two forefingers and thumb of the right hand. They were Dutch sailors, who had been convicted of swearing falsely and had been punished in this dreadful fashion.

Joseph and his companion now faced the problem of getting back to the United States. After some time they found a Danish ship, which took them to a port in Prussia, where an American captain allowed them to continue their journey in his ship, which was bound for Belfast, Ireland. On reaching that port, they waited again for a vessel traveling to Liverpool, England. From that port many ships sailed each year for the United States, and Joseph had no doubt that he could find one which would carry him. It was with high hopes of soon seeing their native land again that they stepped ashore in Liverpool. Little did Joseph realize that it would be more than five years before he would see his father and mother again.

Chapter Three

His Majesty's Sailor

T HE warm spring breeze blew softly as Joseph Bates and his friend wandered up and down the docks of Liverpool one afternoon in late April. The fifteen-year-old cabin boy who had shipped out of New York was now an experienced sailor nearing the age of eighteen. Now that the dangerous adventures through which he had passed the previous winter were over, Joseph was eager to return home. His parents would no doubt be greatly worried by his long absence, as he had not been able to send them any word. Day after day they continued their search for a westbound ship.

There seemed to be ships in the harbor from all over the world. Time after time Joseph stepped up to the commanding officer and asked courteously, "Whither bound, sir?"

For a while, all the answers were discouraging—Buenos Aires, Constantinople, Sydney, Montreal, Cape Town.

Then one afternoon he found a captain who in reply to his question replied with the magic word "Boston." "Could you not use a couple of extra hands on your homeward voyage?" asked Joseph. "Surely I could," the man replied. "Come down in the morning, and I will sign you on."

That same evening, while sitting in the common room of their boarding house, the lads were startled to hear a loud pounding on the front door. A stern voice shouted, "Open in the name of the king!"

Hastily unbarring the door, the landlord stood back, watching an officer accompanied by twelve soldiers enter the room. They made up what was called a "press gang" in those days, and their work was to go around looking for strong young men, whom they seized and forced into the king's navy. When questioned, Joseph and his companion showed their American identification papers, but the officer brushed them aside, and the two were hustled away to a place where they could be guarded through the night.

The next morning they were marched through the main streets of the city to the dockside. Here they were placed in a small boat and rowed to the *Princess*, a ship of the Royal Navy. Up the ladder they were forced to climb. They were then led into a large room on the lower deck where they found about sixty other Americans, who were likewise being pressed into the service of the English government.

Feeling that their imprisonment was unjust, the men plotted to escape. When the officers of the ship went ashore to attend a funeral, the Americans cut the bars which covered the porthole and were just preparing to drop into the sea when the officers returned and the plan was discovered. Many of the older men were given severe whippings for this, but Bates was not one of them. The next day the *Princess* sailed away to Portsmouth, a seaport on the south coast of England, where they were transferred to the *Saint Salvador del Mondo*.

Bates and one of his companions determined to make one last effort to escape. They realized the dangers which would face them as they tried to swim the three miles to shore, encumbered by their clothing as they would be. However, they felt that no risk would be too great if only they could escape from the British Navy. After Joseph had tied his shoes around his neck, first he, and then his companion, was lowered with rope through the porthole by one of their friends. It was nearly midnight, and only a few lights could be seen on the distant shore. But alas! An alert sentry happened to spot them and gave the cry, "Man overboard!" Lanterns were brought and a boat lowered which began to circle the warship. For a time the swimmers remained under the surface whenever the boat came near. Realizing that this could not go on long, they surrendered and were hauled dripping from the sea and marched up the deck to the commander's cabin.

"Who are you?" demanded that officer, angry at being disturbed at such an

Unbarring the door, the landlord stood back. An officer and his soldiers—a "press gang"—were looking for strong young men to seize and force into the king's navy.

hour.

"An American, sir," Bates replied.

"How dare you try to swim away from this ship? Don't you know you might have been shot?"

"Since I am not a subject of King George, I do not wish to serve in his navy, and my only desire is to regain my liberty," Joseph replied.

"Silence!" roared the officer. "I will see that you have no further opportunity to escape. Here, sentry, take this man down to the lockup and put him in irons."

After spending thirty hours in close confinement, Joseph was transferred to the warship *Rodney*, which was just leaving for service in the Mediterranean. As he was marched onto the deck of the ship, her commander was handed a slip of paper stating that Bates had already made two efforts to escape from service.

"Scoundrel," muttered the officer, giving Bates a black look.

So the *Rodney* sailed away that day with Joseph Bates a most unwilling member of her crew. It did not take him many days to learn that a sailor's life in the Royal Navy in the year 1810 was neither happy nor comfortable. The hours of work were long, the tasks hard and often dangerous, the food monotonous— bully beef, hard biscuits, and a ration of fiery grog. Every violation of the rules of the ship was severely punished.

A little more than a week after they left England, the *Rodney* arrived at Gibraltar, where the ship took on fresh stores and then steered into the Mediterranean. Here they encountered one of the most dreadful storms which Bates had ever seen. The gigantic waves rolled the ship in a most frightening manner. For three long days and nights there was no rest for anyone.

One afternoon, far away in the distance, Bates saw the outlines of many ships. "What are those ships?" he asked one of the sailors on deck.

"Those are British warships belonging to the fleet. There are thirty of them, and we are going to add another one, or we will replace one being sent home for repairs."

"What are they doing there?"

"That is the Mediterranean Fleet blockading the French ships shut up in Toulon harbor."

"How long will we have to remain here and guard them?"

"Who knows?" laughed the sailor. "As long as this war lasts, I suppose, and it has been going on now for fifteen years. Nobody seems able to beat 'Boney's' army on land, and he has been afraid to fight on the sea since we licked his fleet at Trafalgar Bay." "Boney" was the name the British gave Napoleon Bonaparte, the emperor of the French.

Little by little Joseph became used to the service. He learned to handle the guns, to stand watch, scrub down the decks, polish the brasswork, and do the hundred odd jobs requiring constant attention on a man-of-war. One bright Sunday morning he heard an officer on deck give a sharp order:

"Strike six bells there!"

"Aye, aye, sir," replied the sailor on duty.

"Boatswain's mate!"

"Aye, sir!"

"Call all hands to church! Hurry them up here."

The mate went below to hurry the men to this appointment, a piece of stout rope swinging from his hand with which to encourage the tardy ones. He came to Joseph, who was watching to see what was going to happen. Recognizing him as a newcomer, the mate asked him:

"To what church do you belong?"

"I am a Presbyterian, sir," Joseph replied, as that was the church into which he had been baptized as an infant, although actually he had never joined any church.

"Only one denomination here—away with you to the kings' church."

With a heavy heart Joseph ascended the ladder and joined the hundreds of men standing on deck. Most of the sailors held small Church of England Prayer Books in their hands. The service was read from the book by the commanding officer. Every now and then the whole group of men responded in unison:

"O Lord, incline our hearts to keep thy law."

"Poor sinners!" thought Joseph. "How little they know about the law of God. Six days a week they are cursing and swearing and drinking; then on Sundays they attend a service like this."

The long, dreary months slipped by. The days grew shorter and shorter, and the nights, especially to those on watch, seemed so long. The wind blew icy cold, and it was difficult to keep warm in the light uniforms offered by the navy. During the winter storms the ships tossed about for days on end. It had been months since Joseph walked on dry ground. He had long talks with the other Americans serving on the *Rodney*. It was difficult not to feel bitter as they thought of home and loved ones. Bates wondered whether the two letters which he had been permitted to write to his parents had ever reached them. If not, they must surely think him dead by now.

There was one subject about which the sailors talked constantly, all of them. That was the day when their ship would be ordered back to England. Once every three years each ship was returned to Portsmouth for inspection and repair. When that joyful time came, every sailor would receive his accumulated pay and twenty-four hours liberty on shore in which to spend it.

"If I ever get on shore," muttered Joseph to himself, "nobody will ever see me again on one of the king's ships. They will never catch me a second time."

When another dreadful storm fell on the fleet, some of the ships were ordered to the island of Minorca. Here it was found that ten of them had been so greatly damaged that they must return to England for repairs. One was the *Rodney*. It was wonderful news to the sailors.

"Homeward bound!"

"Twenty-four hours liberty!" Joyous shouts were heard on all sides. Every heart was glad. Then one evening, just after dark, the very day before the *Rodney* was to leave, some fifty of the sailors were called by name on deck and ordered to get their baggage ready and prepare to leave. Joseph was one of them, so he went down to his cabin, got his meager belongings, and returned on deck. When all of the Americans were again on deck, they were ordered into two small boats.

"Where are we going?" asked Joseph of one of the officers whom he had come to know quite well. "Why are we leaving the *Rodney*?"

"Do you see that ship over there?" asked the officer, pointing to another warship which could be dimly seen in the gathering darkness. "That is the *Swiftshore*, and you are being transferred to her."

The spirits of the men sank. The *Swiftshore* had just arrived from England and was scheduled for a three-year term of service. Poor Bates felt very downcast. It was evident that the officers had not forgotten how he had tried to make his escape while in Portsmouth, and they would not trust him on shore. Was he going to spend the rest of his life in the service of King George?

Chapter Four

His Majesty's Prisoner

M R. BATES sat in his office in New Bedford one day, looking over some bills of lading covering a shipment of goods which had just arrived in port. There was a rap at the door.

"Come in," called out the merchant.

The door opened, and a personal friend entered, carrying a letter in 'his hand, which he thrust across the desk.

"Did you get this for me in New York?" Mr. Bates asked.

"That's right. I knew how glad you would be to get it, for to me it looks as if it came from over the water. I know how worried you have been about Joseph."

With trembling hands Mr. Bates took the letter and unfolded it. The hand-writing told him that it was indeed from Joseph, the son from whom he had heard nothing for more than two years. This was the first and almost the only letter which was to make the long journey from a British warship in the Mediterranean to the quiet Massachusetts town. The letter, written shortly after Joseph had been taken into the British Navy, told of his impressment and appealed to his father to try to secure his release.

Leaving his office, Mr. Bates hastened home to share the news with his wife. Surely it was good news to know that their son was not dead, even though it made them sad to hear of his unfortunate experience.

"Prudence must hear about this," remarked Mrs. Bates. "I will run over and tell her as soon as I have finished the baking. Poor girl, she has been grieving for Joseph for a long time now."

Prudence Nye was a village girl for whom Joseph had formed a strong attachment before leaving on his ill-fated voyage to Russia. She had been faithful to his memory, declining all attentions of young men in the village. She never lost faith that she would see him again.

"He'll come back, Mrs. Bates, I know he will," she had repeated over and over again.

Before the sun went down that afternoon, Mr. Bates had talked with a close friend about the steps he should take to secure the release of his son from the British Navy. He wrote a letter to President Madison himself, mentioning his own war record and asking that documents be prepared and sent to him which could be used to prove to the British government that Joseph was an American citizen and the government in Washington desired his immediate release.

The mail moved far slower in those days than it does now, there being no public service. More than three weeks passed by before Mr. Bates received an answer from the White House. The president was happy to do all he could, and the documents Mr. Bates had requested were enclosed. A few more weeks and these same documents were put into the hands of Captain Delano, a man from New Bedford making a voyage to Minorca himself, who readily offered to place them before the British authorities there.

Captain Delano's voyage was successfully completed, and he had the privilege of laying the documents with a letter from the American government in the hands of Sir Edward Pelew, the commander-in-chief of the Mediterranean Squadron. He in turn communicated their contents to the captain of the ship on which Joseph was serving. Of all this, of course, Joseph knew nothing. One afternoon he was called before the captain.

"Is your name Joseph Bates?"

"Yes, sir."

"Are you an American?"

"Yes, sir."

"To what part of America do you belong?"

"New Bedford, in Massachusetts, sir."

'The Admiral is inquiring to know if you are on board this ship. He will doubtless send for you. You may go now."

Joseph could not conceal his pleasure, and the word spread fast among his mates that he was an American whose government was demanding his release.

But weeks and months rolled by, and he heard nothing more of the matter. By the late fall of 1812, Joseph had been two and one-half years with the Royal Navy. When his ship put into Port Mahon in the Minorca Islands for the usual winter repairs, Joseph took advantage of his twenty-four-hour shore leave to call on both the American and British consuls. The American consul informed him that apparently the admiral had done nothing about his case; and since war had now been declared between England and America, there was no possibility of his immediate release. This was bitter news to Joseph, whose hopes had been raised so high.

Back on board his ship, the *Swiftshore*, he talked over with the other twenty-two Americans on the vessel the significance of the news he had heard and what it meant. They readily admitted that their British masters could force them to fight with the French or Turks or any other foreign nation, but they were not going to fire British guns in a war against their own country.

In a group the men went to the first lieutenant and requested that from henceforth they might be considered as prisoners of war and treated as such. The matter was referred to the commander-in-chief who gave orders that this was to be granted, not only to this group, but to all the two hundred Americans at that time serving with the squadron.

Eight dreary months of inaction followed. They remained on the ships, and constant pressure was put upon them—unsuccessfully in every case—to get them to renounce their American citizenship and join the British Navy.

When their captors found that no impression was being made, the government ordered that they be taken to England. A special ship was chosen, and all the Americans were transferred to it. Passing through Gibraltar, they crossed the Bay of Biscay, sailed up the English Channel, and at length dropped anchor in the Thames River some seventy miles below London. Here they were put on board a regular prison ship, the *Crown Prince*. Other impressed seamen joined them until they numbered more than seven hundred. Their quarters were crowded and the food was neither plentiful nor appetizing, but the long hours with nothing to do was the worst feature of their stay there. They felt that somehow they had to keep in touch with world affairs and know how their country was faring in the war. They could hope for no release until it was over.

Once a week the prisoners received a small ration of salt fish. A plan was made by which they sold this back to the contractor and handed the money thus obtained to one of their guards who secretly purchased for them copies of the London papers. In this way they were able to follow the progress of the war, rejoicing in every American victory, and cast down by each defeat.

The prisoners had not been on board long before they began planning to escape. With nothing more than a common table knife, they set to work to make a hole in the side of the ship large enough for a man to slip through. This task took them nearly forty days. They had to work with great caution, not daring to make any noise, for directly over the place chosen for the hole the sentry paced back and forth all night long, only stopping now and then to send out his reassuring cry, "All's well!"

The night finally came when everything was ready for the escape. In order to divert the attention of the guards, the prisoners began singing some popular American folk songs. As the guards and even the sentinel paused to listen to the lusty singing, one prisoner after another was safely pushed through the hole into the sea and made his way to the nearby shore. This continued until eighteen men had been sent off. Swimming through the black water toward the shore, the swimmer could hear the cry of the sentry proclaiming that all was well, reassuring him that his escape had so far not been discovered.

When the hour became late, the prisoners decided not to arouse suspicion by singing longer. Tingling with excitement, they covered up the hole and lay down to sleep, dreaming of further escapes the following night.

At ten o'clock that night everything was ready for the escapes to begin again. Unfortunately two of the prisoners who had been drinking insisted on going first. Fearing that if they thwarted them they might become so rowdy as to arouse the guards, the other prisoners allowed them to go. Unluckily the second man out was not much of a swimmer and sank deeply into the sea. Coming to the surface, he began splashing and struggling for life.

Fearful that a sound may betray them, desperate men launch a daring attempt to escape-even within sight and hearing of the sentry who paces back and forth directly over their escape hole.

The sentry on duty nudged his companion.

Fearful that a sound may betray them, desperate men launch a daring attempt to escape-even within sight and hearing of the sentry who paces back and forth directly over their escape hole.

"Here's a porpoise," he said.

"Put your bayonet into him," was the next suggestion.

"I will if he comes up again."

The prisoner came to the surface again, kicking and gasping. There was a rush, followed by a loud cry, "Don't kill me! I am a prisoner."

"A prisoner! Where did you come from?"

"Out of the ship."

The soldier raised a shout. "Help! Help! The prisoners are escaping through a hole in the ship."

Guards rushed on deck. The thunderstruck commander hastened from his cabin, a lantern in his hand. Opening the hatch, he rushed down the ladder shouting:

"What's going on here? How many have escaped?"

One of the prisoners, wishing to have a little fun at the officer's expense, replied, "About forty, I guess." The commander nearly fainted.

A large troop of soldiers were quickly rowed to the shore and told to scatter out and search the surrounding woods thoroughly and pick up as many escaped prisoners as possible. But the Americans had been gone for twenty-four hours and were now many miles away. Not one was retaken. Two weeks later the commander received a letter from one of the escaped men in London, telling him that all eighteen were on the point of leaving England aboard a foreign ship, and promising not to return.

The morning after the escape the captain examined the hole made in the ship and sent to Chatham for some of the king's carpenters to come and make the necessary repairs. This they did from the inside of the ship, taking all day doing it. While the carpenters were busy on one side of the hull, several prisoners picked up tools left lying around and promptly proceeded to the opposite side, where they made another hole as large as the first. The soldiers on deck above took it for granted that all the noise was being made by the king's carpenters.

The new hole had been cut very rapidly through a copper plate which had left sharp, jagged edges. To protect the one going through, a blanket was wrapped around those edges. All was now ready for the next escape attempt. Far more caution would be needed now, for the commander was on the alert.

All night long he had two sailors rowing a boat around the *Crown Prince* with orders to raise an alarm on seeing anything moving in the water. By timing this boat, the prisoners were able to judge just when it would be on the opposite side of the vessel. Choosing an opportune moment, one man slipped into the water, looked around, and said that the prospects were good if they timed it right. In order that a large number might go, it was decided to postpone the escapes until the evening.

Alas! all their high hopes were dashed. Someone carelessly left the blanket sticking out of the hole, and as soon as it was light, the sailors in the rowboat raised a shout:

"Another hole on this side of the ship!"

The commander came rushing out again, fearing that more of the Americans had gotten away. A quick count of the prisoners calmed his fears. But he was beginning to have serious misgivings. As things were going, he was sure that sooner or later those Yankee prisoners would succeed in sinking his ship or making their escape. He declared that he would rather take charge of six thousand French prisoners than six hundred Yankees. He wrote to the Admiralty and urged that his prisoners be moved to some safer place. On learning the facts, their lordships agreed with him.

Early in 1814, all the prisoners were sent by sea to Plymouth, a seaport on the south coast of England. From there they were marched overland to a place called Dartmoor.

"Where are we going?" one of the prisoners asked the guard.

"To Dartmoor Prison," was the unsmiling reply. "Let us see if you can escape from that place."

As they came in sight of that massive prison with its thick walls and cold stone buildings, capable of holding many thousands of men, Joseph's heart sank. The darkest days of all lay just ahead.

Chapter Five

Freedom at Last

"MORE prisoners coming." Once again the news traveled swiftly through the gloomy Dartmoor Prison one morning about three months after Bates and his companions had passed through its massive portals.

With one of his friends, Bates made his way to the entrance, watching to see who might be arriving this time. Almost every week a new batch of prisoners had come through the doors to join the thousands of Americans already captured in the war. Most of them had been taken in America and were being transferred to England for safer keeping. "Hello, Sam, where did you come from?" one of the prisoners called out to one of the new arrivals whom he recognized.

"Marblehead," the man replied, a smile breaking over his face.

"Any more left?"

"No, I was the last one."

By this they found out that nearly every sailor from Marblehead had gone to war.

With autumn came a chill in the air. The days grew shorter and the nights colder. Joseph lay close to his companions in the large common room, where hundreds slept on the hard stone floor with only a thin blanket to keep them warm.

With one of the prisoners, Davis by name, Joseph became particularly friendly. They spent many hours talking together relating their varied experiences during the war. Both of them had noticed the terrible effects which strong drink had on their fellow prisoners. Clasping hands together, they pledged themselves to live a life of temperance when they should once more take their places among men in free society.

One icy December day a rumor swept through the prison like wildfire. Peace between the United States and England had been signed in Ghent, a small city in Belgium, and that meant that they would soon be released. But was it true? The guards confirmed the report. On reflection, however, the men realized that as the American Senate must ratify the treaty before it could go into effect, it might be many weeks before they heard anything further. A dreadful thought came to them—suppose the Senate refused to ratify? Sadly Joseph and his friends had to recognize that it might be many weary weeks before they were finished with iron bars and prison fare.

Two months later, in February of 1815, good news came again. The treaty had been ratified. Now surely, they thought, we will soon depart from this dreadful place. Shouts of joy rang through the gloomy halls and echoed down the long corridors. The very thought of being free, entirely free once more, after spending so many years subject to the orders of others, was a thought too wonderful for words.

But still they were not released. As days stretched into weeks and weeks into months, the tempers of the prisoners became frayed. Governor Shortland, a British naval officer caring for the prisoners, was a stern and forbidding man. He decided to change their food ration, giving them hard ship biscuits instead of the soft bread they had been receiving.

"We will accept it," said the prisoners, "providing we are given the same weight of biscuits as that of the bread we have been receiving."

"No," replied the governor, "the biscuits are more concentrated, and the weight will be reduced by one third."

"To that we cannot and will not agree," replied the spokesman for the prisoners. For two days they refused to accept any food unless it was kept to the previous weight. The exasperated governor threatened to withdraw all water if the prisoners did not accept the rations offered. Just at this point in the controversy he was called away for a few days, and a lieutenant remained in charge.

By the third day the prisoners were in an ugly mood, and when ordered to return to their rooms for the night, refused to go unless they were fed. The perplexed officer wondered what he should do.

"Return to your cells immediately," he commanded.

"Not until we have our food," was the defiant reply.

"If you do not return immediately, I shall be obliged to order the soldiers to fire on you."

"Fire away! We would as soon be dead from bullets as from starvation."

Being both humane and kind, the lieutenant, regardless of the orders of the absent governor, commanded that the full ration of food be given to each man. Satisfied, the men returned to their cells.

Upon his return the governor heard what had happened and became very angry. He declared that he would get revenge. Soon his opportunity arrived. A few nights later as he waited with a troop of soldiers in the main courtyard, a weakened gate against which the prisoners were crowding while passing to their rooms gave way, spilling them out onto forbidden ground.

The governor shouted, "Fire!" The guns spoke. Seven men fell dead, and more than seventy others lay bleeding on the pavement while the rest of the prisoners made desperate efforts to avoid the whistling bullets.

This affair made a great stir, and a strong protest was lodged. A court of inquiry was set up which blamed the governor, and the British government agreed to pay compensation to the widows of the dead men.

Now spring had come. Warmth was in the air and hope in the hearts of the prisoners. One evening as they were receiving their rations, the British officers informed them that they would be set free the next morning. This time there was no mistake. On April 27, 1815, Joseph Bates with some seven thousand other prisoners tramped through the gates of Dartmoor to freedom again. As Joseph thought back to the hour he was taken, he suddenly realized that it had been exactly five years to the very day since he had been impressed into the Royal Navy in Liverpool. Half of that time he had been a sailor on His Majesty's ships; the rest of the time he had been a prisoner.

The American consul in London arranged for 260 of the released Americans to return home on the British ship *Mary Ann*. Joseph was one of this group. As they slipped down the Thames River, they passed a long line of warships withdrawn from active service. There lay the *Rodney* and *Swiftshore* on which Bates had for more than two years worked and suffered. Cheer after cheer went up as the Americans saw the foreign coastline disappearing behind them. Homeward bound!—it was a wonderful feeling!

With the prow of their ship turned westward, the released prisoners rejoiced at the thought that each day brought them nearer home and loved ones.

"Ever see any icebergs around here?" one of the sailors asked Joseph.

"I surely have," he replied. "In fact my last ship ran into one in the middle of the night in this very area." Some of the other sailors mentioned how they had also seen icebergs.

"This is the most dangerous season of the year," one of them remarked. "I think we should warn the captain and urge him to be careful."

When they approached Captain Carr, he only jeered at them. "I have made fifteen voyages to Newfoundland," he sneered, "and never once have I seen any ice."

That night the wind was blowing strongly from the northeast, and by nine o'clock a gale was whistling through the rigging. The captain refused to take in any sail, and the ship flew along at tremendous speed. About thirty of the Americans placed themselves around the sides and prow of the vessel, all intently watching the sea. Around midnight they noticed that it was growing colder and concluded they were nearing ice. They knew that should an iceberg be seen in front of the ship, there would be no time to furl the sails before striking it. In desperation and alarm they made their way to the captain's cabin and pounded on his door. Captain Carr stuck his head out.

"Please, sir, take in sail."

"No!" The captain barked out the word. "I thought we had settled that."

"Sail is going to be taken in either with or without your permission," one of them shouted, shaking his finger at the captain.

Realizing from the grim looks on the faces of the group at his door that he was really powerless in the matter, he yielded and gave the desired order. During the rest of the night the ship moved gently up and down on the waves.

As the sun came up the next morning, they were horrified to see tremendous icebergs scattered over a wide area of the sea. Carefully the ship was steered through. The captain had no comments to make.

"Where are you going to land us in America?" they asked him one day as they realized they were off the coast of Maine.

"I have been chartered to put you down at City Point, Virginia, where there is a load of tobacco waiting for me."

Since nearly all of the Americans were from New England, this was disappointing news indeed. After discussing the matter among themselves, they determined to defy the captain a second time. Taking command of the ship, they steered her into the harbor of New London, Connecticut. News spread fast through that little seaport town that a ship with prisoners had arrived from England, and virtually the whole community came out to welcome them. Some of them were reunited with their absent loved ones that very day.

Joseph here found a ship which took him around to Boston, where a friend of his father lent him thirty dollars with which he bought some decent clothing. By stagecoach he completed the journey to New Bedford. With a light step and joyful heart he made his way to the old home to receive a wild and delirious welcome from his mother, father, brothers, and sisters. To Joseph this was one of the supreme days of his life.

Friends and neighbors dropped in to welcome him home, full of questions about his experiences during the years he had been away. But it was to the family circle that evening that he talked for hours, detailing his trials, first in the navy and then in the terrible prisons in Europe. By Joseph's special request, Prudence Nye joined the family that night, following with the closest interest everything Joseph said. As he related the long story of his sufferings, he saw tears trickling down some cheeks. He then endeavored to change the subject to more pleasant happenings.

It was near midnight when the little circle broke up. Walking with Prudence along the quiet street to the home of her parents, Joseph realized that some of the anxieties which had tormented his heart while he was in Dartmoor Prison had been unnecessary.

They paused at the gate of her home, and he gently took her soft hand in his. She looked up into his face.

"Joseph, I am so glad you came back. I knew you would."

"Prudence, I cannot tell you how thankful I am to be back and to find you here to welcome me," he replied.

There was no need to say more. Each understood the unspoken thoughts of the other. The twinkling stars looked down upon them.

Joseph and Prudence paused at the gate of her home. As the twinkling stars looked down, each understood the unspoken thoughts of the other.

Chapter Six

Back to the Sea

"WELL, son, have you not had enough of the sea now?" Father Bates put the question squarely to his twenty-three-year-old son one morning not long after Joseph had returned from his six-year absence in Europe. Joseph returned his father's gaze steadily as he replied slowly, carefully weighing every word:

"No, Father, I haven't. That is the only work which I am really qualified to do. I have learned no other trade. In spite of all the misfortunes which befell me, I still love the sea. I must sail again."

So a few weeks later when a former schoolmate approached Joseph with an invitation to sail with him as second mate on a voyage to Europe, he gratefully accepted. Little did he dream of how long the voyage would take or what manner of trip it would be. They first went to Alexandria, Virginia, where the vessel took on its cargo for Bremen, Germany, and then sailed away.

Late in October they reached their destination and began the long task of unloading. Just as they were taking out the last few tons, a sudden cold snap came on, ice twenty feet thick formed on the river, and the ship was locked in its frozen grasp all winter. In the spring when the ice broke up, they found that the ship had been seriously damaged. Considerable time was taken in making repairs, so it was midsummer before they recrossed the Atlantic and tied up again in Alexandria.

Every voyage served to increase the confidence and trust which his superiors placed in Joseph because of the good judgment he always showed in times of danger. At the end of 1816 he was named first mate of the brig *Criterion*, which first sailed to Boston, picked up a cargo for Baltimore, there unloaded, and reloaded a different cargo for New Orleans. By this time it was January in one of the most bitterly cold winters in the history of the eastern states.

At dawn on a gray day the *Criterion* pushed out of Baltimore and made its way down the Chesapeake Bay. The captain and Bates both noticed ice forming fast on the surface of the bay. Remembering what ice had done to his former ship in Germany, he urged the captain to get clear of the bay as fast as possible and move out into the open sea. Together they both made their way to the pilot, who was standing on the bridge.

"Do you think we can get clear of the bay before it freezes over?" they asked him.

"No, I expect to anchor here near the shore and push on in the morning," the pilot replied.

"That will be too late," remarked Mr. Bates. "The ice will form during the night, and in the morning we shall be unable to move."

Having worked as a pilot around Chesapeake Bay all his life, the man refused to listen. The anchor was dropped, and all hands except the regular watchman turned in for the night.

During the night the tide went out, grounding the ship on a low mud bank with ice forming fast all around the vessel, which suffered serious damage from its constant battering. When daylight came again, they saw that it would be necessary to cut the ice away from the anchor chain in order to raise it, before they could hope to be free. As Joseph and four or five of the crew were doing this from the ship's rowboat, the wind suddenly caught them, the ice began to move, and in spite of their best efforts, they were driven, at first slowly, then more and more rapidly, down the bay until they lost sight of the *Criterion* altogether.

The hours of the short winter day slowly went by. An icy wind was blowing, and none in the boat had brought extra warm clothing with them. They were entirely without food. So far as Joseph himself could see, there was no hope of saving their lives, but like a wise leader, he kept such thoughts to himself. Human beings simply could not live long in such bitter cold.

As the black night closed down on them, they could see, seven or eight miles away on the Maryland shore, the lights of a few farmhouses; but one by one these were put out as the hours of night passed by until all were dark. About nine o'clock the ice began to break away, and they were once more in open water, where they could use their oars. They rowed as rapidly as they could toward the shore, which they knew lay to the west of them.

After rowing for four or five hours against both wind and current, their boat struck a sandbank, perhaps three hundred yards from shore. One of the men leaped into the water, waded ashore, and began to search for a house. He returned before long, shouting the welcome news that he had found a house and the family were making a fire.

It was agony leaping into the icy water, but it had to be done. One by one Bates counted his men, but didn't see Tom, one of his best seamen.

"Where's Tom?" asked Joseph, peering about in the darkness. "There he is, lying in the bottom of the boat," replied one of the sailors.

Joseph shook him, but he seemed to be dying of the cold.

"Where am I?" he asked at last as Joseph continued his efforts to arouse him.

"Come, come," urged the mate, "get out of the boat and follow us!"

Together the miserable group waded ashore and stumbled along the narrow path to the farmhouse. There they found a roaring fire which had been prepared for them. The half-frozen sailors rushed up to it and were soon groaning in agony as the frost came out of their hands and feet. Joseph refused to get near the fire, but rubbed his limbs with snow, thus thawing them out gradually. As a result, he was the only one of the party who did not suffer permanent injury from the terrible experience they had passed through.

When morning came, Joseph borrowed a horse from the farmer and rode it back to Baltimore, where he informed the owner of the *Criterion* what had happened to their ship. A salvage crew was sent to see what could be done, but it was found that the battering the ship had received from the ice had damaged it beyond repair. By heroic efforts they managed to recover most of the cargo, but the ship itself had to be abandoned. The owner later managed to sell it as scrap for twenty dollars.

Once again Joseph was back in Baltimore looking for a ship. His skill and resourcefulness had been so outstanding on the *Criterion* that he was now made first mate on another ship, the *Francis F. Johnson*, which was carrying a cargo of dry goods to be sold in South American ports. This voyage was extremely successful, and Bates was able to return to Baltimore with very large profits for the owners of the vessel. The manager was so pleased with what Joseph had done on this voyage that he gave him a handsome reward of several hundred dollars. With a light heart Bates took passage on a coastal steamer for Fairhaven, where he once more had an opportunity to relax with his family. Fairhaven was that part of the New Bedford community lying east of the bay. It had separated from the older town during the War of 1812, and the parents of Bates had their home in Fairhaven.

Not long after his return, he called on Prudence Nye. This time he brought up the subject which was uppermost in his mind.

"Prudence," he said, taking her soft hand into his rough, calloused one, "will you marry me? I love you with all my heart. You are the only girl I have ever wanted; and now I want you more than ever. "

"Joseph," replied Prudence softly, "you know my heart is yours. I have waited for you for many years. I will gladly marry you. But, Joseph, tell me one thing. Do you expect to spend all of your life on the sea?"

Joseph's face became sober. "No, dear, I do not expect to do that. It is a hard life, and it has always seemed unfair to me for a man to expect a wife to remain so many months of every year without seeing or hearing from her husband. But I am convinced that I can make my fortune on the sea within a few years. I promise you that when I have accumulated a fortune sufficiently large so we shall never be in danger of suffering from poverty, I will leave the sea and seek some other line of employment."

"Joseph, please don't be cross with me, but tell me just how much you expect to get before you call it a fortune?"

"Frankly, Prudence, I have thought I would like to have around ten thousand dollars."

Prudence was satisfied. On the fifteenth day of February, 1818, the two were married. Six weeks later Joseph returned by sea to Baltimore to make arrangements with his former employer to serve as first mate on a ship sailing for Europe during the summer.

Chapter Seven

Perils of the Deep

G OOD-BY, dear. Take good care of yourself, and please remember to send me word if you have an opportunity after you reach Europe." Joseph Bates kissed the upturned face of his wife of only a few months.

"Good-by, Prudence. I do not think we shall have any difficulty on this voyage. The ship is new and the crew experienced. If all goes well, we should be tying up here again by the end of September, well before the beginning of the winter storms."

The sun shone bright and warm that beautiful June day in the harbor of New Bedford as Joseph Bates stepped aboard the good ship *Frances Hitch*, with cargo bound for Bremen. As second in command to Captain Hitch, Joseph felt a personal responsibility for her success. Briskly he now gave orders to the sailors, and before long the graceful vessel was under way with beautiful, billowing white sails.

In early August after an uneventful voyage across the Atlantic, the ship anchored and the cargo was profitably sold. Then they proceeded to Gottenberg, Sweden, where the work began of loading hundreds of heavy iron bars which were to be taken back to the United States. As part owner of the ship, Captain Hitch was eager that as large a cargo as possible should be taken on board. Certain it is that the ship was overloaded, but the captain and first mate anticipated a speedy return to New Bedford, and their vessel supposedly would ride all the steadier for being well laden.

Never were seamen's hopes more rudely disappointed. Sailing through the

North Sea, they ran into a very untimely snowstorm. Rough seas caused the ship to labor heavily, and they blamed the many dangerous leaks which opened up along the keel of the vessel on the heavy cargo of iron. In order to steady her, the crew brought up twenty tons of metal and lashed it on the main deck, but this only helped temporarily. The chief cause of worry to the officers and men arose out of the direction of the wind, which blew from the west without ceasing day after day.

The *Frances Hitch* had no motors to propel her through the sea against the wind, so it was almost impossible to make any progress. Two, three, four weeks went by as they battled forward little by little, tacking first to the north and then to the south as they zigzagged their way across the cold Atlantic.

As the days stretched out, they became seriously worried about their dwindling supply of provisions. Their food was running out, and only a limited amount of water could be given to each man daily. In an attempt to make their ship ride better, the twenty tons of iron on deck were thrown overboard and a similar amount brought up from the hold.

Then one day, to their great joy, the wind veered around to the east, and for a while they made excellent progress. "Three more days of this and we shall tie up in New Bedford harbor," said the captain one evening. Even that would mean a ten-week voyage from Gottenberg, which would be almost twice as long as it should have taken.

But they were not to reach New Bedford in three days—no, not for three months. About midnight a tremendous gale arose. In all the years he had spent on the sea Joseph Bates had never seen such a sea as they saw at dawn on that cold November morning. The sails had to be furled in the teeth of a wind that did its utmost to pull the men from the mast and hurl them into the foaming seas. Mr. Bates reported the situation to Captain Hitch.

"Keep the ship dead before the sea!" he ordered. "That is our only hope."

All day the storm raged. With the coming of darkness the wind seemed to increase in fury, if that were possible. Wave after wave battered the ship, apparently coming in from all directions. The second lot of iron was sent hurtling overboard, making the ship lighter by another twenty tons. The second morning of the storm dawned with the rain descending in torrents. Between seven and eight o'clock the wind stopped suddenly. For a few minutes there was a

43

dead calm, then the gale struck the ship from the opposite side. An instant turn of the rudder was made to save it from turning over. The ship became quite unmanageable. It mounted up to the crest of enormous waves, then literally fell into the troughs between them. The captain came on deck, gave one horrified look, and exclaimed, "Oh, my grief!" and for a time remained silent. The ship was leaking in a dozen different spots. Pumps were being worked continuously. It appeared as if the end had come.

With the exception of the captain's young son and his nephew, whom it was feared might be swept off the deck by the furious wind and waves, all the crew not working the pumps gathered on the pitching, tossing quarter deck.

"Cook, can you not pray for us?" shouted the captain, striving to make his voice heard above the shrieking of the wind. The Negro cook and the captain were the only two professing Christians on board.

The cook then knelt down on the pitching deck and offered up a short but very earnest prayer entreating God to save them all from the raging storm. Sinners as they knew themselves to be, Joseph Bates and his associates were confident that the cook's prayer, although apparently snatched away by the howling gale, was heard by the Master of wind and wave.

All that day the storm continued to rage. It seemed a miracle that the ship could continue to climb up and down the mountainous waves. The captain and Bates agreed that the ship could not endure much longer the terrible battering she was receiving. The leaks had increased, and the pumps were working twelve thousand strokes every twenty-four hours.

On that very night when it seemed that the crisis had been reached, Prudence Bates was visiting at the home of a relative a few miles from her home. While she was there, a Methodist minister called to visit the family. Prudence seemed unusually sober, and he asked her for the reason. She pointed to the windows against which the rain was being dashed, driven by a fierce wind.

"I greatly fear for my husband, whose ship is long overdue in New Bedford," she replied. "If they are exposed to the fury of this storm, they may be in great danger."

"I want to pray for that ship's company," replied the minister, and they knelt together. His fervent prayer made such a deep impression on Mrs. Bates that she jotted down (in the journal which she always kept) a record of the event. When Joseph finally reached home more than three months later, they sat down together and compared records and found that the minister's prayer had been offered on the night of his own greatest danger.

By this time the food supplies on the *Frances Hitch* were completely exhausted. About midnight the lookout discerned the lights of a vessel directly ahead, steering toward their stricken ship. When within hailing distance, the two vessels exchanged information concerning their respective names and destinations.

"Can you spare us some provisions?" called the *Frances Hitch.*

"Yes, as much as you want. I am loaded with them," replied the other ship.

"Lay by, and we will send our boat," replied the officer on the *Frances Hitch.*

Bates and the sailors began to unfasten the lifeboat and prepared to launch it. The captain's heart sank as he watched them. Was there any hope of reaching the other ship? he wondered. Could any lifeboat float in such a sea?

"Mr. Bates, I dare not have you go," said the captain. "To lose some of the crew now would be very discouraging, and how could the ship be saved in her leaky, sinking condition?"

"Captain Hitch," Joseph replied, "this is our only hope. We will all die of starvation unless food is found. You know we are out in mid-Atlantic, many hundreds of miles from any land."

The captain in silence turned away. Bates called for volunteers, and three seamen were found willing to risk their lives along with their gallant mate.

The lifeboat was dropped into the sea, the men tumbling down the rope ladder into it. The captain, with a 'prayer in his heart, committed them to their perilous ride over the mountainous waves to the other ship, which they safely reached. Several barrels of bread and flour were dropped down to them, and by efforts which left them completely exhausted, they succeeded in reaching their own vessel again.

These provisions nourished them for some time. But storm after storm buffeted them and drove the disabled ship far from its course. Then, just in time, they met another vessel and bought more food and water, then a third, a fourth, until in all they had received help seven times.

Still the westerly wind blew until it was evident to the captain and Joseph

Bates that there was no hope of reaching New Bedford that winter. So they turned southward and steered for the West Indies. After many more weeks of tossing, they at length entered calmer waters and eventually anchored in the harbor of St. Thomas, a seaport on one of the Virgin Islands. Here the ship was completely overhauled. The masses of barnacles and grass which had collected on the keel were removed. They were then ready for the final lap of their journey up the coast of the United States.

All of their dangers, however, were by no means past. Off notorious Cape Hatteras they met a particularly violent storm which they successfully outrode and against contrary winds inched their way up the coast. When only two days out of New Bedford, the gallant ship faced one last attack from all the marshaled forces of the sea. This forced them to run into a sheltered harbor in Vineyard Sound near New York City, where they remained at anchor for three days.

The wind subsided, and on the twentieth of February, 1819, they dropped anchor in New Bedford harbor, six months after leaving Gottenberg, Sweden. Never did wives give a more tumultuous welcome to husbands, many of whom they had long since given up for lost. Thus ended the longest and most dangerous voyage ever undertaken by Joseph Bates.

Chapter Eight

Along the Temperance Road

OR a number of months following the terrible voyage on the *Frances Hitch*, Joseph Bates remained at home with his family. He was then invited to take the position of second in command on another ship, the New Jersey. It was with sad misgivings that Prudence saw her husband prepare to leave home again to face the dangers of the sea; yet she made no objections, realizing that the sea life was the only one he knew and that in spite of its perils, he found it a truly thrilling one. Besides, she was proud and happy to know that after every voyage, Joseph was able to add something to the fortune he was gradually accumulating and thus bring nearer the glad day when he could retire from sea life.

For the next eight years, Joseph sailed almost continuously. His first voyage was to Europe, where he delivered a cargo of salt which his ship had taken on at Bermuda. On his return from this trip Bates was offered full command of the ship *Talbot*, sailing out of Salem for Liverpool. From this time on he was Captain Bates to the officers and crew of all ships he was to sail. The *Talbot* made a successful voyage to England, returning safely to Alexandria, where it unloaded cargo. Not finding anything further to do immediately, Bates returned to visit his wife in New England, having been absent this time for sixteen months.

In 1821 Captain Bates again took command of the *Talbot*, sailing from Alexandria again, this time loaded with a cargo of flour for South America. Such was the confidence of the owners of the ship that they left it to the judgment of Captain Bates to decide where and when to sell the flour. Bates and his sailors voyaged southward until the *Talbot* dropped anchor, first at Rio de Janeiro, where part of the flour was sold, then at Montevideo, where they disposed of the balance. Then back he went to Rio de Janeiro for a cargo of hides and coffee, and from there they returned safely to Alexandria.

It was on this voyage that Joseph Bates took the first steps along the health reform path. For many years he had lived on shipboard with noisy, drunken officers and sailors. These men, when drunk, filled him with disgust, and he had long before resolved to hold himself to a very small amount of strong drink, never more than one glass of grog each day. But he became alarmed when he found that he was looking forward to that small glass more than to anything else in the day. This caused him to ask himself whether there was not a danger that in time he might allow himself to take more than one glass. As a result of his serious consideration of this question, he startled the men at his table one day by announcing with firm determination:

"Gentlemen, I have drunk my last glass of strong drink!" This was a renunciation of only strong liquor. He continued for some time to partake of light wines, ale, and beer.

The owner of the *Talbot* had such confidence in his captain that he bought a fast new ship for Bates to take around Cape Horn into the Pacific, giving him a free hand to trade there. When Captain Bates returned to Baltimore and saw the new ship, he was delighted. There was something else in the city, however, which brought him sadness. With a letter from his wife in his hand, he went to see the director of the company for which he worked.

"I regret to inform you, sir," said Mr. Bates, "that it will not be possible for me to sail before returning from a visit I must make to my home in Fairhaven. My wife has informed me in a letter, which was awaiting me when I arrived, that our small son passed away while I was gone. I must go and see her immediately."

"You have my sympathy, Captain Bates," replied the man. "As it will take several weeks to complete the work of fitting out the *Chatsworth*, you may take whatever time you think you need for this visit. The ship will be waiting for your return. "

Bowing, Captain Bates left the office. By stage coach, the fastest means of travel, he returned to Fairhaven for a brief visit with his wife and his father and mother.

When returning to Baltimore a few weeks later, Joseph Bates and six other passengers were entering the city of Philadelphia in a stage late at night. As they were crossing a dry gully, the straps fastened to the driver's seat broke, and the two men on the box were pitched off the stage, falling dangerously into the path of the wheels. They passed over the hand of one man, crushing his fingers, and took the hat off the other. The passengers inside the coach awoke with a feeling that they were traveling at great speed.

"Why are the horses going so fast?" asked Joseph Bates.

"Don't know," replied one of his companions.

"Let them go," said another. "I like to go fast."

But Bates had an uneasy feeling that something was wrong. He opened the coach door and called to the driver, but, of course, received no answer. Peering up from the step on which he stood, he saw through the darkness that the coach was driverless and was dashing madly down Third Street. In places, Joseph could see large banks of snow which had been shoveled back off the street; he speculated whether he should try jumping into one. The other passengers were now urging him to jump so they could get out of the heavy coach before it upset or ran into one of the narrow bridges, as by this time every traveler was aware of his peril.

At length Joseph jumped, pitching forward onto his head and rolling over several times. The heavy wheels missed him by only a few inches. The result of the fall was a cut on the top of his head, which bled fast for a few minutes. As the stage continued rattling down the street, the other passengers managed to jump out without serious injury. Not long after, the coach ran into one of the bridges and was totally wrecked. Thanking God for his deliverance, Joseph found another coach to Baltimore.

It was now 1822. Captain Bates stood once more at the wheel of a ship bound for the open sea. Southward they proceeded day after day, stopping now and then after they reached South American ports, where they were able to dispose of various parts of their cargo. In the harbor of Buenos Aires they stopped while the ship was made ready for the rough and dangerous voyage around Cape Horn. It was while traveling between Buenos Aires and the Horn that Captain Bates decided to drink no more wine or ale. The officers at his table and even the crew poked fun at him for this decision. When he pointed out that there never could be a drunkard if all followed his example, they agreed that his course was perfectly safe, although they themselves had no desire to adopt it.

As this voyage took Bates farther down into the Southern Hemisphere than he had ever gone before, he had time and opportunity to study the heavens and learn the names of many stars which are not visible in the northern sky. As captain, he had to know how to chart the course of his ship from the position of the heavenly bodies. The more he learned of the heavens, the deeper became his interest in astronomy. From this time on he read every book or scientific paper on the subject he could obtain.

The passage around Cape Horn, which took the ship through the famous Strait of Magellan, was difficult at any time of the year, while rounding it in winter as Bates and his crew did was worse than usual. For days the wind blew steadily against them from the west, and the seas ran high, but in the end they succeeded in reaching the Pacific side of South America. Here in the harbors of Chile and Peru, Captain Bates disposed of the balance of his cargo most profitably. He did more than that—he did what few captains would think of doing. Being offered $10,000 for the *Chatsworth*, he accepted and arranged to return to the United States on another vessel.

While waiting to sail, Joseph Bates attended a banquet to which all Americans were invited on February 22 in honor of the birthday of George Washington. Mr. Swinegar was an American merchant living in Peru, who handled the business for the company employing Joseph Bates. At this banquet an embarrassing scene arose when the host requested all present at the table to pour out a glass of wine and drink a toast to their country and its founder. When Bates filled his glass with water, he was firmly but politely requested by the host to replace it with wine. Bates just as firmly but politely refused, and for several minutes there was a warm argument, but in the end, as the captain remained firm, Mr. Swinegar gave way.

It was after his return from this banquet, that same night, that Captain

Although the officers at his table poked fun at him, Captain Bates was firm in his decision to drink no more wine or ale.

Bates made another important decision. From henceforth he would smoke no more cigars. He still continued to chew for a short time.

On the good ship *Candace*, commanded by Captain Burtody, Joseph Bates sailed for the United States after spending more than a year trading in the Pacific. Captain Burtody was an old friend of Bates, and they passed many hours in pleasant conversation. Before setting sail, Joseph Bates and Captain Burtody agreed that when the ship weighed anchor they would from that hour cease chewing tobacco. The evening they left South America they were sitting on the upper deck watching the stars come out as they cleared the last landmark of the harbor of Valparaiso, starting on their 8,500-mile voyage home. The steward came to announce that dinner was served.

"Here goes my tobacco, Bates," said Captain Burtody as he threw his plug into the sea.

"Here goes mine, too," responded Captain Bates, following suit. From that hour he kept the resolution he made that night never to touch tobacco in any form again. Unfortunately Captain Burtody went back to his tobacco within a few days.

"There is another habit which I have yet to conquer," said Bates to himself, "and that is the sin of profanity." From his earliest days as a cabin boy on his first ship, all through the years, he had heard cursing and swearing daily. From hearing it, he had taken to using bad language himself. He now became convinced that it was wrong and resolved to try to stop. Perhaps if he had had a greater knowledge of God, he would not have taken His holy name so often in vain.

It was on this voyage that Bates began the habit of reading a chapter or two from the Bible every day. By so doing, he concluded that he was making himself into a pretty good Christian. Poor Joseph! It was going to take him a long time to discover that nobody can make himself into a Christian.

Week after week slipped by with the ship slowly creeping up the coast of South America, across the Caribbean Sea, and then along the eastern seaboard of the United States. One morning the joyful cry, "Land ho!" rang through the ship. There lay Block Island, only forty miles from Boston. The pilot boat came alongside.

"Where are you from?"

"The Pacific Ocean."

"Whither are you bound?"

"Boston."

"Will you take a pilot through Vineyard Sound?"

"Yes, come alongside."

Soon the pilot was clambering on board and taking over the wheel. The sailors could not restrain their curiosity and began asking questions.

"What's the news in the States, pilot?"

"What's the news from Europe?"

"Who's going to be our next president?"

"Have you any newspapers?"

"Yes, but they are four days old."

"Never mind. It has been nearly two years since we saw an American newspaper. It will all be fresh news to us."

As soon as Captain Bates had reported to the owners of the *Chatsworth* and handed over the money he had brought back from her sale, he took the stage for Fairhaven. To him those fifty-five miles seemed the longest of the entire journey. The question always arose in his mind: How will I find my family? Has God spared their lives while I have been away?

Prudence Bates was in the front yard when she glanced down the street and saw her husband approaching. To his great surprise he saw her turn and run up the steps of the house and disappear inside. A few moments later she came out bearing a young child in her arms. Who could it be? wondered the bewildered husband. Then in a flash the truth came to the delighted father as he held out his arms and took a beautiful blue-eyed baby girl from his wife's hands. She was sixteen months old, and it thrilled him to hold his little daughter and look into her sweet face for the first time. The little girl was not so pleased, but pulled a sad face and began to cry, not knowing who this stranger might be. Joseph understood and with a hearty laugh handed her back to Prudence.

The lights burned late in the home of Joseph Bates that night as husband and wife sat together relating the various events which had happened to each during the two years since they had parted.

53

Chapter Nine

Not Far From the Kingdom

"WELL, Bates, where do you go this time?"

Captain Bates was standing on the New Bedford wharf, watching the sailors making last minute preparations to sail. He turned to his friend and smiled.

"I expect to be back in South America within six weeks. This is the finest ship I have commanded yet," he said, pointing with pride to the beautiful three-masted schooner named the *Empress*, tied up to the pier.

"Do I understand correctly that you are part owner of this vessel?" continued his friend.

"Yes," Joseph Bates replied, "I have a half interest in her, so will have a right to 50 per cent of any profits I make while trading in South America."

Two hours later the vessel, with sails fully set, scudded before a favorable wind out of the bay onto the broad Atlantic. A fast trip brought them to Richmond, Virginia, where they took on a cargo of flour. Leaving here, they next stopped at Norfolk, where Captain Bates had expected to pick up a cannon. Few vessels sailed the seas in those days without some armament as protection from pirates, who still roamed the ocean. Not finding a cannon available, he was forced to sail without it. Out on the open sea again, he turned the prow of the *Empress* southward, bound for Brazil.

The days grew warmer as they traveled farther and farther toward the tropics. With plenty of leisure time again, Bates proceeded to unfasten the sturdy trunk which stood in one corner of his cabin.

"I wonder what I will find to read first," thought the captain to himself as he lifted the lid. During his months on land he always picked up quite a supply of the latest novels and romances to read during the long hours at sea.

"Hello, what's this?" he murmured to himself as he picked up a neatly bound copy of the New Testament which Prudence had placed on top of the other books. "Evidently Prudy thinks I read too much light literature."

Sitting down, he immediately began to read from the Testament, a Book of which he was at the time almost completely ignorant. Several weeks later he was to make mention of the event in his journal which he kept so faithfully on all of his voyages, pointing out how his interest in novels had ceased from that day. He was not yet a Christian, although he had a secret longing to become one, could he only be sure of the steps he ought to take.

One afternoon he was aroused by a knock on his cabin door. "Come in," called out the captain. One of the sailors entered.

"How is Christopher?" asked Captain Bates, feeling sure that the sailor's errand had some connection with the condition of one of the seamen who had been ill for more than a week.

"He is dead, sir, I am sorry to report," replied the sailor.

"I am grieved to hear it," said the captain. "See that the usual preparations are made for his burial." The sailor went out, leaving Bates to his thoughts. He was troubled, deeply troubled. It was his responsibility to conduct the burial service for the unfortunate seaman. How could he, who was not a Christian, offer a prayer in public? The very thought overwhelmed him.

Feeling that he must make some contact with God, Joseph Bates now retired to a secret hideaway he knew of, where he would be safely hidden from the eyes of the non-Christian officers and men of his ship. Here he bowed on his knees to pray . Years later he told of how it seemed to him that every hair on his head was standing straight up, so awesome was the thought that he, a poor sinner, was actually addressing the mighty God of the universe. His great problem at this moment was how he could offer up a public prayer for the soul of the poor sailor.

Shortly after returning to his cabin, he was informed that everything was ready for the burial. The body had been sewed up in canvas and weighted, ready to be slipped into the sea. Still the captain could not bring himself to offer a prayer; yet he did not wish to bury the man without a service of some kind.

"Excuse me, sir," someone whispered into his ear as he stood before the assembled sailors. "Would you like to use a Prayer Book of the Church of England?"

Captain Bates turned and saw the steward.

"Oh, yes. Do you have one?"

"Yes, sir."

"Please bring it at once."

In a few moments the steward handed him a copy of the English Prayer Book. He had not looked into one since leaving the British Navy fourteen years before. From this book Captain Bates now read the burial service for the dead.

The burial of this sailor made a deep impression on Bates. Suppose it had been he instead of poor Christopher who had disappeared into the blue depths that day. What kind of account could he render to his God? Before leaving New Bedford on this voyage, Captain Bates had talked about conversion with some of his friends who were church members. Through what kind of experience would a person pass before he could claim to be converted? They assured him that he would probably feel a great burden of sin, and these feelings would last for two or three weeks. If he continued to pray, the Lord would come and speak peace to him, and he would lose this burden. Captain Bates felt the burden, but in spite of the prayers which he now offered up daily, the feeling that he had been really converted did not come.

Arriving at the harbor of Pernambuco, Brazil, Captain Bates disposed of most of his cargo. Here he learned of a drought which had been raging for two years, and that the country behind the city was on the brink of revolution because of the existing famine. He immediately decided to secure a load of farina, that being one of the chief articles of diet in Brazil at the time. With this in mind he sailed for St. Catherine, where he secured a good supply and returned to Pernambuco. The authorities of the harbor, however, refused to allow him to sell it.

"Do you not know," they asked him, "that no vessel not owned by a Brazilian may engage in trade between two ports of this country?"

This information threw Bates into great perplexity, as he did not know what to do with his cargo. However, within a few days word came from the head of the government of the province, stating that he would be happy to buy Bates' entire supply for his troops. In view of the famine they would even give him written permission to import another load. This trade proving very profitable, Bates remained in that part of South America for nearly a year, making many voyages in which he transported food to the starvation areas.

Once when he came to the port of St. Catherine, the local merchants, knowing what he wanted, decided to greatly increase the price. However, he outwitted them by sailing along the coast some miles to a small cove where he anchored his ship. Here he went ashore with an interpreter and several members of the crew to carry the heavy bags of money with which to buy the farina.

Coming to a farmhouse where there was an abundance of flour for sale, he entrusted his bags of money to the farmer for safekeeping through the night. Bates found, however, that he could not sleep, for the horrifying thought suddenly struck him that the farmer might kill him during the night and enrich himself with the money. His fears were groundless, for in the morning the farmer not only sold him a large quantity of flour, but expressed gratitude for the confidence Captain Bates had shown in him.

This trading voyage was most profitable for Captain Bates. It was with a feeling of real satisfaction that he loaded a cargo of hides and skins and headed once more for his homeland in the North. Late in March, 1826, after an absence of twenty months, his good ship *Empress* entered New York harbor to unload her cargo.

Leaning over the rail one morning, watching the dockmen carry the cargo onto the pier, Joseph Bates was startled to see a familiar figure. He puzzled for several minutes trying to identify the man before it suddenly came to him that it was Davis, who had shared his prison cell in the Dartmoor Prison twelve years before. Bates hastened forward and made himself known to the astonished Mr. Davis. A few inquiries and each knew of the station in life attained by the other. To his deep regret Captain Bates learned that Davis had failed to

57

keep the resolution he had made in the prison to steer clear of alcoholic drink, but had allowed his appetite to ruin his life.

The contrast between the two men was startling. There was Joseph Bates, captain and half owner of a beautiful ship, owning his own home and having several thousand dollars in the bank, drinking cold water and enjoying perfect health. Mr. Davis was a day laborer, picking up whatever jobs he could, suffering from a terrible cough and poor health in general, a self-confessed slave to alcohol. Captain Bates regarded the difference in their stations in life as one of the rewards of his own temperate life.

A light ship and a brisk wind gave the *Empress* a fast voyage to New Bedford, where she tied up at the same pier from which she had sailed away nearly two years before. Joseph Bates was delighted to find how much his family had grown during his absence, although to the children he seemed almost a stranger. He was saddened to note how much his father had aged during his absence, but he listened with pride as the old man told of the visit in the previous year of his one-time commander, General Lafayette, when the gallant French general revisited the United States.

"Yes, my son, I am sorry you were not here to meet him. He came to Boston, and I was among the many who had the privilege of shaking his hand. He recognized me instantly and thrust out his hand, exclaiming, 'How do you do, my old friend, Captain Bates?' Someone standing nearby asked the general, 'Do you know him?' 'Certainly, he was under my immediate command in the American Army.' I should greatly have enjoyed introducing him to my son."

One evening not long after he reached home, Prudence brought up the subject which had been much on her mind during the long months of separation.

"Joseph, have you been converted? Are you now a professed Christian?"

"Prudy," he answered slowly, "I really do not know."

His wife seemed very much disappointed. "But did you not read the New Testament I placed in your trunk? Have you not been praying? Did you not confess your sins and ask for forgiveness?"

Joseph admitted that he had done everything she mentioned.

"Then why aren't you sure that you have been converted?" persisted his wife.

"It seems to me," he replied, "that in a matter of this kind one must be absolutely sure. I have had no wonderful feelings of joy or other deep emotions."

Not many nights later the pastor of the Congregational Church invited Joseph to attend a religious meeting where various members of the church would tell of their conversion experiences. Bates agreed to attend the meeting only on condition that he not be called upon to speak. As he listened to the new Christians outlining the simple way in which they had confessed their sins and accepted by faith the pardon offered, he was astonished. If that was conversion, then he could be converted. Nay, more than that, he was converted already. He said to himself:

"Is this conversion from sin? Is this really it? Then I have experienced the same," and his spirit burned within him, leading him to wish he also might testify.

From that night on, all doubts left Captain Bates, and he rejoiced in the blessed assurance of full salvation in Jesus.

He now determined to publicly join the church, but the question arose, Which one? His parents were members of the Congregational Church and had been all their lives. His wife, to whom he owed so much, was a member of the Christian Church.

In keeping with his cautious nature, Joseph carefully examined the fundamental beliefs of the two churches. The most outstanding point on which they differed was in regard to the mode of baptism. Where the Congregationalists sprinkled their converts, the Christian Church immersed. After fully examining the Bible teaching on the subject, Joseph decided that immersion was the only mode taught and so was baptized and joined the Christian Church. When her loving husband proceeded to erect the family altar in their home, Prudence Bates felt that her cup of joy and blessing was running over.

Chapter Ten

Farewell to the Sea

O N THE same day that he was baptized, Joseph Bates spoke to the minister of the Christian Church he was joining, inviting his help in forming a temperance society. For personal reasons, the minister declined to lend his name to the project, and Bates moved out alone. He drew up a paper pledging the signer to abstain from the use of all intoxicating drink and to use his influence in turning others from its use also.

Feeling very much embarrassed, Joseph Bates first took the paper to the Congregationalist minister whose church he had declined to join because it did not immerse its candidates. To his surprise and delight, the minister agreed immediately.

"Why, Captain Bates," he exclaimed, "this is just what I have been wanting to see," and he signed the paper.

With this good beginning, Bates next took the paper to all his friends and acquaintances around the town. Although some of them laughed at him for his pains, a number joined, and thus there came into existence the first Fairhaven Temperance Society, almost the first of its kind in America.

At first the use of wine, beer, and cider was not prohibited, until one day a member of the society was seen drunk on the street. At the next meeting the matter was drawn to the offending member's attention.

"You were drunk, and this will give our society a bad name if it continues," one of his fellow members said.

60

"I was not drunk!" the man protested. "How could I be drunk when I had taken nothing stronger than hard cider?"

"If you drank nothing stronger than hard cider and still got drunk on it," they replied, "then that also must come under the ban."

Since the man had broken the spirit if not the letter of the rules of the society, he was expelled, and their rules were amended so as to forbid drinking anything containing alcohol sufficient to cause intoxication. From this time on they were known as teetotalers. A little later they organized the children of the town into a group by themselves, which became known as the "Cold Water Army." It gave Joseph Bates great pleasure when more than three hundred children joined this army in the New Bedford area alone. More joined in other towns and cities.

Almost a year and a half passed from the time Joseph Bates returned on the *Empress* till his next departure on what was to prove his last voyage. During that time his brother had taken the ship to South America and returned with excellent profits, which they shared. Another cargo was now placed on board, and on August 9, 1827, the ship set sail once more. Captain Bates was finding it increasingly difficult to bid farewell to his wife and children.

On the first day at sea the captain called all the sailors together, except the man at the wheel, and spoke to them concerning the voyage before them. There was to be no swearing on board, nor were any intoxicating drinks to be brought onto the ship at any time. If any of the crew could not agree to these conditions, the captain offered to put in at the next harbor and let him go. Although some of the men grumbled that it would be hard to stop swearing, not one refused to accept these regulations. As they sailed on together, Captain Bates did everything in his power to make it a pleasant voyage for them all. Every morning the crew was gathered into the main cabin, where the Bible was read and prayers were offered. A large supply of Christian literature had been taken on board, and copies of the paper Zion's Herald were handed out each Sunday.

Arriving at St. Catherine once more, the *Empress* tied up, and within a few days the whole cargo had been sold, and the hold was bulging with fresh farina and rice. As the ship was preparing to sail for Rio de Janeiro, eight Brazilian gentlemen approached the captain and offered to give him fifty dollars each if he would carry them to the capital city. Bates agreed, took their money, and with their personal belongings safely on board, they set out together.

With a favorable wind the ship made a fast voyage. Early one afternoon the dim outline of Sugar Loaf and other high peaks surrounding the harbor of Rio de Janeiro came into view, although still nearly eighty miles away. Suddenly a strange craft was seen approaching at great speed.

Captain Bates put his spyglass to his eye and saw that the ship was being propelled not only by the wind which filled her ample sails, but also by long oars which were seen dipping into the sea, causing her to nearly double her speed. As a result, the strange ship rapidly overtook the *Empress*, and as she approached, she began firing her guns at the American ship. In order to identify himself, Captain Bates hoisted a large American flag, but the strange ship continued to approach and fire until the *Empress* took down all sail and stopped. As the ship drew near they could see it was from Buenos Aires, as it was flying the Argentine flag. The Brazilian gentlemen were greatly troubled.

"Oh, what shall we do? What shall we do?" they repeated over and over again. They were greatly agitated because of the state of war existing between Brazil and Argentina at the time.

As it was evidently an enemy ship with a lawless crew, the sailors and passengers alike were worried about how much they might lose in the coming search. The Brazilian merchants were particularly anxious and began running to and fro looking for a safe place to conceal the small fortune they were carrying in gold pieces.

As they hurried through the galley, the men were urged by the cook to throw their money into the great pot filled with beef and pork, bubbling and boiling on the stove. This they gladly did, and the gold pieces quickly settled to the bottom. The *Empress* was lying still in the water when the captain of the pirate vessel drew near, cursing and swearing, and ordered Captain Bates to come on board his ship. Bates appealed to the captain not to allow his men to loot the *Empress*, but was told that the men had been promised this privilege as a reward for rowing hard.

The marauding sailors were then turned loose on the *Empress*. They ransacked the ship from stem to stem, searching for money and valuables. Naturally, none of them ever thought of looking into the big pot boiling on the stove. But they did carry away rich plunder in the shape of clothing, watches,

The strange vessel rapidly overtook the Empress and began firing her guns. In order to identify his ship Captain Bates hoisted a large American flag.

and other valuables.

When the looters returned to their own ship, laden with the things that they had taken, they brought with them the eight Brazilian merchants. Captain Bates immediately spoke to the pirate commander and asked that the men be released and allowed to continue their journey with him to Rio de Janeiro. The Brazilians, huddled in a group and guarded by one of the sailors, stood together nearby, realizing all too well what their probable fate would be, should they be kept on board the Argentine ship. Were they not citizens of an enemy country? Captain Bates saw the fear written on their faces and determined to make one last effort to save their lives.

Drawing the captain to one side, Bates spoke most earnestly, appealing to his more humane nature. The prisoners, pale and agitated, gazed imploringly at Captain Bates.

"Will you let my passengers go with me?"

"No, they are my prisoners."

"I know that, sir, but I shall be greatly obliged to you if you will let me have them."

"I think that is entirely my own business."

"Please reconsider the matter," urged Captain Bates. "These men paid me fifty dollars each to land them at Rio de Janeiro. I have nothing to lose if you keep them, but I shall feel I have broken my word. They have never injured you, captain."

"Take them, then," said the captain in a subdued tone and with a wave of his hand.

Together with the grateful Brazilians, Captain Bates returned to the deck of the *Empress*. There was great rejoicing on board when once again they could set their sails and proceed. The gold pieces were scooped out of the kettle, and although many articles of value were missing, no lives had been lost. That night they had a prayer and thanksgiving meeting. Captain Bates reported this strange incident to the authorities in Rio de Janeiro. A warship was immediately sent out to search for the strange craft, but it had disappeared.

Several months were then spent transporting cargoes of rice and farina to various ports in Brazil. At length the ship put into the harbor of St. Catherine, where a cargo of hides and skins was taken on board to transport back to New

York. Captain Bates settled in full with the merchant who had sold them most of their supplies. In some way the man undercharged them by five hundred dollars.

Unfortunately this mistake was not discovered until they had voyaged some distance down the river. Bates immediately anchored his vessel and sent the money back with some of his crewmen in a small rowboat. The merchant was greatly surprised and pleased to receive this money.

The efforts which Bates put forth on behalf of the spiritual welfare of his men were not in vain. On the return voyage there was a revival on board, and a number of the sailors were converted.

As the ship neared New York, Captain Bates was both surprised and pleased when a delegation from the crew came to him to tell him how much they had enjoyed sailing with him. They found that they had profited greatly from the experiment of sailing on a "dry" ship and requested the captain to take them with him at any time in the future when he might be making another sea voyage.

The *Empress* arrived in New York, where it discharged the cargo picked up at St. Catherine. Then for the last time under the command of Captain Joseph Bates the sails were unfurled, and the ship scudded before a favorable breeze up the New England coast. Homeward bound! This time it was to be the last return trip for Joseph Bates. During this voyage, more than on any of his previous ones, he had thought much on how many of the joys of life he was missing by being away from his wife and children so much. He made up his mind to retire from a seafaring life and give his time to interests in the vicinity of his home.

Captain Bates stood at the wheel of his ship as she glided up the New Bedford roadstead, gazing through the bright afternoon sunlight for first glimpses of old familiar landmarks. He well knew that word of his coming would soon spread through the small town.

"Mother! Mother! Father's ship is coming into the bay!" Joseph Bates, Jr., rushed into the house with the joyful news. A smile lit up the face of Prudence Bates as she picked up her little girl and with her only son made her way to the wharf to welcome home her long-absent husband. In a way she had been dreading this meeting, even though she knew it had to come. How was she to break the sad news she had for Joseph?

As the *Empress* drew up at the pier, Joseph studied the faces of his loved ones. He noticed how the children had grown, how neatly his wife had them dressed. Joseph leaped ashore and gathered his family into his arms. But his wife's bearing told him that something was wrong.

"What is it, Prudy?" he asked. "What are you troubled about?"

"Joseph, your father passed away a month ago."

Chapter Eleven

Behold He Cometh!

JOSEPH, wake up. I think the house is on fire!"

Prudence Bates shook her husband, and in a moment he was awake—wide awake. The room was as bright as day, yet the old clock on the mantel showed only two o'clock. Joseph, springing out of bed, hurried to the window.

"Oh, how wonderful! How beautiful! Prudy, come quick and see."

Prudence joined her husband at the window. As far as the eye could see in every direction, stars were falling to the earth as thick as rain. Dressing quickly, they stepped outdoors. Never had they seen anything like it, a perfect snowstorm of falling stars.

"I think I know what this means," remarked Joseph. "Do you remember in Matthew 24 the account of Jesus giving His disciples many signs in order that they might know when His coming was near? One of those signs was that the stars should fall from heaven. Then there is a verse in Revelation which describes just what we are looking at. Prudence dear, fetch the Bible."

In a few moments his wife returned and placed the large family Bible in her husband's hands. She watched as he turned to Revelation, the sixth chapter, and read the thirteenth verse. The words stood out, clearly illuminated by the light from the blazing heavens.

"And the stars of heaven fell unto the earth, even as a fig tree casteth her untimely figs, when she is shaken of a mighty wind."

"Do you really think, Joseph, that we are seeing the fulfillment of that prophecy tonight?"

"I have not the slightest doubt of it."

It was the night of November 13, 1833, five years after Captain Bates had finally left the sea. Joseph and his wife were not the only ones to witness the falling of the stars that memorable morning. Thousands of others, all over the land, saw it and recognized it as a sign of Christ's second coming. Many tracts were written about it, and hundreds of sermons in the weeks that followed called the attention of Christians everywhere to this great sign.

The years since Joseph Bates retired from the sea had slipped by pleasantly. There were three daughters in the home now, but still only the one son. We know little of the family life of Joseph Bates, as he did not write on that subject, but knowing he was a kind Christian gentleman, we may be sure his was a happy home. He kept himself busy advocating the cause of temperance and rejoiced as hundreds of societies sprang up all over New England.

Another cause into which he threw himself heart and soul was that of the abolitionists. These were people who were convinced that the whole system of slavery as it existed in the Southern states was wrong and that all slaves should immediately be set free. Joseph Bates joined one of these societies and attended many of their meetings.

When his mother passed away a few months after his father's death, Joseph inherited the ancestral farm near Fairhaven. On this farm he lived for three years with his wife and children. He was not what might be described as a particularly successful farmer, but there were always sufficient fruit and vegetables for his family and some to sell. Then, selling the old home place to his brother, Bates purchased land nearby and began to build a residence and farm buildings. For a short time he experimented with raising mulberry trees and cultivating silkworms, hoping to develop an industrial school, but this industry did not prosper in New England.

One afternoon as Bates was busy in his orchard, an acquaintance called upon him. He was a preacher in the Christian Convention.

"Good afternoon," the neighbor said. "Are you interested in attending a special lecture in New Bedford tonight?"

"What is the lecture about?"

"The second coming of Christ."

Bates asked if he thought he could show or prove anything about the

Saviour's coming.

"I think I can," was the reply. "Will you come and hear me?"

"Yes, I will come, and my wife, also, if I can persuade her to accompany me."

So that evening Joseph and his wife attended the meeting. The speaker was a follower of an Adventist preacher by the name of William Miller, who had been proclaiming the soon coming of Christ for seven or eight years.

In a clear, ringing voice the speaker introduced his subject by reading Daniel 8:14: "Unto two thousand and three hundred days; then shall the sanctuary be cleansed." In Bible prophecy, the speaker explained, a day stands for a year. By studying the prophecy of the seventy weeks found in Daniel 9, one must conclude that this great prophecy would begin in 457 B.C. The 2300 years, then, would come to an end during the year 1843 or 1844. The sanctuary to be cleansed, the speaker went on to explain, was this earth, which Jesus would purify when He returned the second time. He closed his sermon with a powerful appeal to all present to accept Jesus and prepare to meet Him.

The words of the speaker that night carried conviction to the hearts of those present. Captain Bates and his wife proceeded homeward in complete silence for some time, the thoughts of each centering on this important subject. Joseph was the first to break the silence.

"That surely was the truth!"

Apparently Prudence had been waiting for him to speak and was not too surprised at his statement. She looked at him with a smile as she replied:

"Oh, Joseph, you are always so sanguine." She had always been much more inclined to be slow and deliberate in making changes either in her beliefs or manner of life.

"But, Prudy dear, how can one be indifferent when speaking of so great a subject? I must know more about it."

He immediately bought a copy of William Miller's nineteen lectures on the prophecies concerning the second coming of Jesus. Far into the night he studied them, evening after evening. By the time he had come to the last, there was no longer the slightest question in his mind concerning their truthfulness. A tremendous sense of personal responsibility came over him, and he began to ask himself the question, What can I do to get this wonderful truth to the tens of thousands who do not know it?

First of all he determined to know more about this man William Miller. He felt sure that in the city of Boston he would find those who knew him and from whom he could learn much, so he made a journey there. He was not disappointed, for in Boston he met a young minister, Joshua V. Himes, who told him all about William Miller.

"I met Elder Miller when he came to give a series of lectures here in Boston," Elder Himes explained. "As soon as I heard him, I was sure that he had a true message. Elder Miller has been preaching this message for nine years, but few people know much about him. I am now getting out a paper here in Boston called *The Signs of the Times*, which is being read far and near. I hope that soon there will be hundreds of voices proclaiming this judgment hour message where now there are only a few."

"That is a paper I must have," said Bates as he gave Elder Himes a liberal donation for his work.

"Elder Himes," he went on, "I am not a preacher, but I am going to have a part in spreading this message. It seems to me that everyone who hears and believes it must go out and tell others. If this world is going to last only three or four years, we have not an hour to lose!"

From that day Joseph Bates threw everything he had into the work of spreading the good news that Jesus was soon coming. Soon after this, in September, 1840, Joseph Bates was one of sixteen ministers and laymen who signed the call to a conference of those interested in the second advent of Christ.

In March of the next year Elder Miller responded to an invitation to hold meetings in the Christian church in Fairhaven—the church which Joseph Bates had helped to build and to which he belonged. Even though the church was crowded, Bates felt he could not miss one of the studies. The fortune which he had so carefully accumulated during his seafaring days he now devoted to spreading the Advent Message. At the time when his father's estate had been settled, Joseph's fortune exceeded the ten thousand dollars he had set as his goal some ten years earlier.

"But, Joseph," his wife protested one day when she knew he had sent another liberal donation to Elder Himes to help him publish more papers, "what are we going to do after the money is all gone? Who will take care of us in our old age?"

"Oh, Prudy!" Joseph exclaimed. "That is the most thrilling part of it all. You and I are not going to grow old. Jesus is coming soon to bring us eternal life. Why should we have thousands of dollars left to be destroyed by fire when the earth is cleansed?"

Prudence shook her head. She was far from sure that Jesus was returning in a few years. Realizing, however, that she was no match for her husband in argument, she quietly let him go his way. After all, she reasoned, he is a good man and has always provided well for his family.

Out from Fairhaven Joseph Bates now began traveling to neighboring town and villages, speaking to all who would listen of the "blessed hope" as he called the good news that Jesus was coming soon. Sometimes he held meetings in churches or schoolhouses but more often in the homes of farmers when a few families would gather to listen to him.

We do not know when he was ordained to the gospel ministry in any particular church, as he has not told us. There can be no doubt that he was called of God to preach the gospel. From this time on we find him spoken of by those who knew him as Elder Bates.

Chapter Twelve

In Search of Slaves

THE Advent Movement, begun by William Miller, quickly spread to many points in New England after 1840. One young minister, James White, carried it on horseback from town to town in Maine. Before long it was being proclaimed in other states as well. Charles Fitch traveled over the mountains into Ohio and Indiana. As they neared the time when they expected Jesus would come, Joseph Bates sold his home and settled all his accounts. He was greatly troubled because no one seemed willing to travel southward to preach the message to the masters and their slaves in that large part of America. The more he thought about it, the more he felt that he himself should go. But he needed a traveling companion.

He slipped around to the home of his blacksmith friend, H. S. Gurney.

"Good afternoon. What brings you around today, Elder Bates?"

"Gurney," Bates replied; "I think someone should take this blessed truth into the states down South."

"Well, why don't you go yourself? If the Lord has laid this burden on your heart, you should go."

"Yes, I think I shall, but I would rather not go alone. Will you come with me? It will mean leaving your family for possibly three or four months."

Gurney asked for a day or two to think the matter over. He was a fine Christian man, fully sharing the faith in the message of the soon return of Jesus. He had a fine tenor voice and often sang in the services at the church.

Gurney decided to go in spite of the danger of being killed. The Southerners would probably suspect them of being abolitionists, folk who believed slavery should be abolished. The slave owners would naturally be suspicious of anyone coming to talk to their slaves. Still they were determined to go. Elder Bates would preach the message, and Gurney would sing it.

In the icy cold of winter they left Fairhaven, but cold weather held no terrors for the captain, who had faced a hundred storms at sea. A rough and dangerous passage brought them to New York City, where they took the train to Philadelphia. Here they rejoiced to find Elder Miller conducting a series of meetings, and their hearts thrilled anew as they listened to his stirring messages.

From here they traveled into Maryland and crossed over an arm of Chesapeake Bay to Kent Island near the very spot where Bates had landed from the *Criterion* more than a quarter of a century before. Entering a small town, they found most of the citizens gathered in the tavern for a meeting. Elder Bates asked permission to hold a service in one of the two meetinghouses in the settlement, but the trustees of both refused to grant permission. The tavern keeper stepped up to Elder Bates.

"Did you say your name is Bates?"

"That's right. Joseph Bates."

"Were you ever shipwrecked near here many years ago?"

"Yes, I think it was in the year 1817 that our ship the *Criterion* ran aground near here."

"I knew it! I recognized your name. You came to my father's home and stayed a few hours. I was a lad only ten years old at the time. If you would like to hold your meeting here in this tavern hall, you are welcome to do so."

Before the town meeting broke up, Elder Bates had announced a meeting for the following afternoon. The hall was well filled at the appointed time. Gurney stepped forward and sang in a fine ringing voice:

> "Lo! He comes with clouds descending,
> Once for favored sinners slain;
> Countless angels, Him attending,
> Swell the triumph of His train;
> Hallelujah! Hallelujah!
> Jesus comes, and comes to reign."

Elder Bates then unrolled his chart, hung it up, and presented in a clear, convincing manner the thrilling message of a Saviour who would come in the clouds of heaven in a few months.

Each afternoon for five days meetings were held. On the last afternoon, in a saloon about two miles away, a rough-looking group of men were discussing the coming lecture. Concluding that the two visitors were abolitionists, they decided to attend and cause a riot which would break up the service. Bates, informed of this, went forward with the meeting undaunted.

Just as Bates finished speaking, a Methodist class leader and one of the trustees who refused to let Bates and Gurney hold their meetings in the church began to denounce the speaker and the message he had given.

"Why," he shouted, "I can put this whole thing down in ten minutes." Bates looked at him and smiled. "Please come forward and do so. We will hear you."

The man came to the front and began to speak, but it soon became evident that he didn't know anything about the subject. Becoming confused, he suddenly turned and shook his fist at Elder Bates, growling:

"We are going to ride you out of town on a rail!"

"We are all ready for that sir," Bates replied. "If you will put a saddle on it, we would rather ride than walk."

The crowd laughed good-naturedly at this witty reply. Then, in a more serious mood, Bates continued:

"You must not think that we have come six hundred miles through ice and snow at our own expense to lecture to you without first sitting down and counting the cost. And now, if the Lord has no more for us to do, we had as lief lie at the bottom of Chesapeake Bay as anywhere else until the Lord comes. But if He has any more work for us to do, you can't touch us!"

One of the men present, Dr. Harper by name, arose and said, "Kent, you know better! This man has been giving us the truth and reading it out of the Bible. I believe it."

Before leaving the hall, Kent himself came up with an apology, heartily shook the hand of Elder Bates, and said, "Bates, come again and see us."

Going on from Kent Island, the two travelers journeyed by foot to Centerville on the eastern shore of Maryland. They traveled in this way so that they

For a copy of the song an old, white-haired slave came up to
Brother Gurney and offered him all the money he had in the world

might meet the slaves while they were at work in the fields. At Centerville they were entertained by a certain Judge Hopper, whom they met at the store. When someone asked where the meeting would be held, Judge Hopper replied, "In the new meetinghouse."

As they visited with the judge that evening, they learned that he owned a number of slaves. He said to Bates: "Mr. Bates, I understand that you are an abolitionist and have come here to free our slaves."

Bates replied, "Yes, judge. I am an abolitionist and have come to get your slaves and you, too! As for getting your slaves *from* you, we have no such intention. We teach that Christ is coming, and we want all of you to be saved."

This seemed to satisfy the judge, and the meeting was held. Deep was the impression made on those who attended, and many tracts were given out.

At Chester, the next town, Elder Bates asked Gurney to open the meeting with a song which he had come to love. Somehow it seemed to express the feelings of the two messengers as they hastened from place to place with the glad tidings. So again Gurney lifted up his voice and sang:

> "I'm a pilgrim, and I'm a stranger;
> I can tarry, I can tarry but a night;
> Do not detain me, for I am going
> To where the fountains are ever flowing,
> I'm a pilgrim, and I'm a stranger,
> I can tarry, I can tarry but a night."

The people listened with breathless interest as Elder Bates presented the message. All around the back of the room, standing out dark against the white wall, stood scores of slaves, drinking in all that was said. They waited respectfully as the white people left, and this gave Bates and Gurney an opportunity to speak with them.

"Did you hear what was said?"

"Yes, Massa, ebery word."

"Do you believe it?"

"Yes, Massa, believe it all."

"Don't you want some tracts?"

"Yes, Massa, please. Want 'em very much."

"But can you read?"

"No, Massa, but young missus or massa's son will read for us."

So the tracts were left in their hands. One of the slaves, an old, white-haired man, came up to Brother Gurney and offered him twenty-five cents, probably all the money he had in the world, for a copy of the song he had heard that night, "I'm a Pilgrim." Gurney felt so sorry for him that he sat down and made a duplicate copy, which he left with him, much to the old man's delight.

Thus Captain Bates spent the weeks and months between the time he became convinced that it was his duty to proclaim the message and the spring of 1844. He would spend a few weeks at home, caring for the needs of his family; then he would go forth on another preaching tour. Steadily as the expected time of the second advent drew nearer and nearer, the Advent preachers worked more tirelessly.

"Fear God and give glory to him, for the hour of his judgment is come," was the message they proclaimed everywhere with enthusiasm.

Chapter Thirteen

From Sweet to Bitter

O NE evening sounds of singing floated out from the passenger lounge on an intercoastal steamer. Curious passengers began to gather from the deck, from the cabins, and from all parts of the ship. They saw, standing beside a large chart covered with various figures and diagrams, two gentlemen singing together.

> "Hear the glorious proclamation,
> The glad tidings of salvation,
> Hear the glorious proclamation,
> Of the Saviour near."

By the time the seventh verse of this rousing Advent song was completed, the room was well filled with curious men and women. Joseph Bates, Bible in hand, stood near the chart and proceeded once more to explain the prophecy of Daniel which seemed to indicate that Jesus would surely return to earth that very year.

Suddenly the wind began to blow, and the ship tossed up and down. A violent storm had risen, and the meeting was interrupted as passengers were informed that the vessel was putting in to a nearby Connecticut port, and they must complete their journey to Boston by train. An hour later many of these same passengers, now on the train, requested Elder Bates to complete the discussion of the gripping subject to which they had been listening on the ship. His study continued till they pulled into Boston.

In Boston once more, Joseph Bates made his way to *The Signs of the Times* offices. To Elder Joshua V. Himes he made a report of his most recent journeys and was cheered in turn to learn of the progress of the message in Maine, in Ohio, and even in Canada. The Advent presses were busy, and thousands of copies of the paper were going out weekly all over the eastern part of the United States.

He was assured that Adventists were firm in their confidence that Jesus would come not later than the spring of 1844. Bible scholars agreed that the Jewish year would end on the seventeenth day of April, 1844. Jesus, therefore, should come before or on that day.

"Solemn thought," mused Joseph to himself as he stepped out of the office and went on his way. "He could come tomorrow! Nay, He could come today!" His eyes swept over the multitudes passing by in the busy, narrow streets. "How many of them are ready?" he asked himself. "Am I ready? Is my family ready?"

One by one the days passed. Finally the seventeenth of April came. More than fifty thousand men and women were hopefully waiting. But Jesus did not come, and they were sorely disappointed. What did it mean? The enemies who had openly scoffed at the message now asked derisively:

"What are you going to do now that your time is past? Why don't you confess your mistake and give it all up?"

"Because the Lord said, 'Wait for it.'"

"Wait for what!"

"The vision."

"For how long will you wait?"

"Until He comes."

So the Advent people waited, wondered, watched, and continued to study their Bibles.

At his home Joseph Bates was as eager as any to learn whether any new light had been discovered which might explain their disappointment. He read every copy of *The Signs of the Times*. One day in July he saw a notice announcing a camp meeting at Exeter, New Hampshire, commencing on August 12.

"Wife, I am going to attend," he declared, shortly after reading of it. "Something tells me that we shall get new light there."

"Joseph, Joseph," murmured his wife, "I hope you are right."

As he traveled to the meeting, Bates seemed to hear the train wheels repeating, "New light, new light, new light."

At first when he arrived on the campground, he found no one with any light not already known. As one of the leading ministers of the Advent cause, Elder Bates was invited to speak. In a rather lengthy sermon he reviewed the experience of the Advent believers in the past and exhorted them to faithfulness. As was natural for one with his background, he compared their work to the progress of a ship at sea, maybe a little off course, perhaps delayed by storms, but sure to reach the harbor soon. He was interrupted by a sister who arose and exclaimed, "It is too late, brethren, to spend precious time as we have since this camp meeting commenced.... The Lord has servants here with meat in due season.... Let them speak, and let the people hear."

S. S. Snow had just arrived on the campground with new light. New light! The words thrilled Elder Bates, who gladly yielded the pulpit to Elder Samuel Snow.

Carefully Snow explained how the prophetic period did not end until the fall of 1844. Just as in ancient Israel the sanctuary was cleansed annually on the great Day of Atonement, so Jesus would come and cleanse the earth by fire on the Day of Atonement, which would fall on October 22, that very year. He called the attention of the people to the parable of the ten virgins, describing how they had all slumbered and slept.

"Brethren," he concluded, "He is corning. We have a message to give to the world. The midnight cry, 'Behold the bridegroom cometh, go ye out to meet him,' must be sounded far and near. We have only ten weeks in which to do our work before the great day comes!"

Elder Bates was satisfied. It was all as clear as day, and he shared in the excitement which ran through the entire camp. As that meeting closed, the granite hills of New Hampshire were ringing with the mighty cry, "Go ye out to meet him!" As the loaded wagons, stages, and railroad cars rolled away through the different states, cities, and villages of New England, the cry was still resounding, "Behold the Bridegroom cometh! Christ our blessed Lord is coming on the tenth day of the seventh month! Get ready! Get ready!"

In Fairhaven again, Elder Bates was eager to share with his wife and neighbors the wonderful news he had heard at Exeter. The following Sunday, Bates with Elder Macomber, who had also been at Exeter, attended a meeting in New Bedford. Here Elder Hutchinson, who had just returned from Canada, was trying to preach, but somehow he seemed greatly confused and at length sat down saying, "I can't preach."

Elder Macomber sprang to his feet saying, "Oh, I wish I could tell you what I have just seen and heard at Exeter, but I cannot," and he sat down.

"I can and I will!" exclaimed Elder Bates. He then proceeded to expound the new light which had come to the believers at the conference. The meeting that morning ended in triumph as plans were made to spread the message, now called the Midnight Cry, far and wide.

"If what Elder Bates has told us this morning is true," commented Elder Hutchinson, "no wonder my preaching sounded like carpenter's chips."

Who can describe the joyful excitement of the next few weeks for Joseph Bates and his companions? They worked early and late, warning sinners and strengthening the hearts of believers in all parts of the state. Day succeeded day as interest in the things of this world faded and they prepared to move to another.

October 21 came. "Tomorrow is the last day," thought Joseph Bates to himself as he turned in once more at the gate of the home where he and his family stayed. He was a poor man now, all his possessions having been sacrificed for the cause. But what did that matter? The next night they would be sitting down with the faithful of all ages at the marriage supper of the Lamb. The crown of life would be placed on their heads, and they would walk the streets of gold.

The day dawned as usual the next morning. Elder Bates, with thousands of fellow believers, watched the sky that day as it had never been watched before. Who would be the first to see that small white cloud, the sign of the Son of man? The day slowly passed, and darkness finally came on. With the passing of the day sank the hopes of God's waiting people. When darkness deepened into night, the believers knew that they had been disappointed again, and a feeling of terrible sadness overwhelmed them. Men, women, and little children cried long into the night. It seemed as if they could never again hold up their heads before a cruel, scoffing world.

The dawn of a new day brought no relief to the hearts of the believers. Bates sat as if stunned, feeling that he never wished to stir out of his house again. Well he knew that the wicked were rejoicing over the defeat of the disappointed ones. Remain at home, however, he could not. Provisions had to be bought. He must make some plans to provide for the needs of his family during the coming winter. He had been so sure he would never need to buy another ton of coal!

Thinking deep and troubled thoughts, Bates walked slowly down the street, hardly noticing the houses he was passing.

"Ha! Captain Bates," called a rough-looking man from the steps of one house. "Why didn't you go up yesterday?" The man laughed heartily.

Joseph Bates passed on, not trusting himself to give an answer.

Chapter Fourteen

A New Cause to Champion

"WELL, Joseph, what now?"

It was a natural question which Prudence Bates put to her companion one morning shortly after that heart-breaking day when he, with so many thousands of other Adventists, had looked in vain for the return of Jesus. Mrs. Bates had never fully shared his absolute confidence that the Master would surely come on October 22. She had deeply sympathized with him in his sorrow, but now she was thinking of more practical things, as she called them, and wondering what the future held for her and her family.

Joseph Bates returned her gaze steadily as he slowly replied, "Prudence, I don't know exactly what I am going to do."

"Do you still look for the soon return of the Lord?" she gently asked.

"Yes, my faith in that event is as strong as ever. I do not know when it will be, but I am confident that it will be soon. You remember the Apostle Paul bids us in Hebrews not to cast away our confidence, for, he says, in a little time He that will come shall come and will not tarry."

"But Joseph, you have now been disappointed twice."

"I know it, dear, but I still believe that He will come soon. Let me read to you the words of courage from the pen of our great leader, Elder William Miller, in the most recent issue of the *Midnight Cry*:

"'Brethren, hold fast; let no man take your crown. I have fixed my mind upon another time, and here I mean to stand until God gives me more light. And that is today, today, TODAY, until He comes, and I see Him for whom my soul yearns.'"

"Well, Joseph, that all may be true, but you know winter is near, and we have made no provision for it."

"That is true, Prudy, and I have not forgotten it. Do you remember that field of potatoes which I refused to dig several weeks ago, as I felt sure we would never need them in this world? I shall dig them now. Our leaders have not forgotten our present condition. Elder Himes has sent out word that the believers must prepare for another hard winter. I know that it must have nearly broken his heart to be forced to send out such a message."

"All right then, what else are you going to do? We cannot live on potatoes alone."

"The Lord will provide," replied Joseph in his usual calm way, seeking to quiet his wife's anxiety.

"That's what you always say," she answered, showing some annoyance. "You are always so sanguine."

Nevertheless Joseph Bates did bestir himself to provide for the needs of his family and found little difficulty in obtaining employment from his friends in Fairhaven and New Bedford. Nor did he neglect to dig his field of potatoes, which he found in good condition.

During the long winter evenings he spent many hours poring over all the literature he could secure which dealt with the great subject ever uppermost in his mind, the return of Jesus and the prophetic periods of time. A mistake had been made somewhere in the Adventist interpretation of prophecy, and he was eager to find what it was.

One morning in early March he returned from the village post office with the mail. In his study he opened various papers which the Adventists continued to publish and for which he had sometimes written encouraging articles. This morning he found one entitled *The Hope of Israel*, and it had been printed in Maine. On the front page he noticed an article by a certain T. M. Preble calling attention to the duty of all Christians to keep the seventh day of the week as the Sabbath.

"Why, that is taking us right back to Judaism," thought Joseph Bates to himself. However, he took his Bible and proceeded to look up the various texts listed in the article. The more he studied, the more troubled he became. Was it possible that he had been worshiping on a day which God had not blessed or sanctified? Not being a man to make hasty decisions, he pondered the question for several days.

Should he decide to keep the seventh-day Sabbath, how would his wife feel? What would she say? What would his friends think of him should he withdraw from fellowshiping with them at their regular Sunday services? The Advent hope had bound their hearts very closely together. It would be sad to leave their company. Last, but not least, he must consider his family. Would he be able to find employment should he refuse to work on Saturday? He had already passed his fiftieth birthday, and it might not be easy to find work.

When Joseph Bates finally decided that the seventh day was the only Sabbath taught in the Scriptures, however, none of these questions carried any serious weight. After a few more days of deep study he resolved to keep the Sabbath, regardless of the consequences. He learned that in Washington, New Hampshire, not far from where Preble lived, there was a small company of Advent believers who had been observing the seventh-day Sabbath for a number of months.

Elder Bates determined to get in immediate contact with them. There were still a number of questions which he wanted answered. Before announcing his decision to his friends, he wanted to be able to prove from the Bible that he was right, so no one could overthrow him.

A few days later on a bright spring morning he boarded the train, which took him up through the New England hills to a small town on the Connecticut River. There he changed to a stagecoach, which took him the rest of his journey and finally deposited him that evening in the town of Hillsboro. In response to his inquiries he was directed to the home of Elder Frederick Wheeler, the first Adventist minister to accept the Sabbath truth. As he neared the house, Bates noticed that there was no light. It was ten o' clock at night, but he walked up boldly and rapped on the front door. Was this not a matter which required haste? How could he postpone the visit until the dawn of another day?

Frederick Wheeler himself, candle in hand, came to the door to see who might be calling at such an hour. Like many other preachers of those times, he was a farmer during the week and a preacher on weekends. Bates introduced himself.

"I am Joseph Bates from Fairhaven, Massachusetts, and I have heard that you are keeping the seventh day of the week as Sabbath."

"That's right," replied Elder Wheeler. "I have been keeping it for nearly a year."

"I would like to talk with you about it," said Bates. "I wish to know every argument which can be found in the Bible in favor of God's seventh-day Sabbath. I am fully convinced that it is the only rest day taught in the Scriptures, yet who knows about it? Why, man, this is a subject which must be proclaimed everywhere!"

"I am glad to hear you say so, Brother Bates," replied Wheeler. "Come inside where we can discuss the matter fully."

The two men sat down and proceeded to talk all night about the Sabbath. Bates took notes of all that Elder Wheeler presented, asked many questions, and in the end became more firmly convinced than ever that here was a truth which was crystal clear. The sun rising over the granite hills of New Hampshire peeped through the window of the Wheeler home and fell on the kneeling figures of two men, who then were dedicating their lives to proclaiming the Sabbath truth to the world.

Around the breakfast table the Wheeler family met "Brother Bates," as Elder Wheeler affectionately called him. After morning prayers the men drove the twelve miles to Washington to the home of Cyrus Farnsworth, another member of the Sabbath-keeping company. There, under the large maple trees in front of the Farnsworth home, those three believers held the first Seventh-day Adventist conference, although that name, of course, was not to be used for many years. Then Bates started for home.

Two days later Elder Bates alighted from the train in New Bedford and started walking to his home in Fairhaven. As he crossed the bridge spanning the Acushnet River, which separated the two communities, he met one of his Adventist friends, James Madison Hall. With a broad smile Hall thrust out his hand in welcome.

"Captian Bates," he said, "what is the news?"

Back came the joyful response: "The news is that the seventh day is the

With a broad smile Hall thrust out his hand in welcome.
"Captain Bates," he said, "what is the news?"

Sabbath of the Lord our God."

A short but animated discussion followed as Elder Bates outlined the principal reasons for his new-found belief. Before they parted, Bates had promised to present the matter to the Adventist believers.

Elder Bates had returned to Fairhaven a confirmed Sabbathkeeper. More than that, he was prepared to be a champion of the Sabbath. It was no easy task for him to break the habits of forty years. Perhaps one of the heaviest crosses he had to bear was the opposition of his wife. To her it seemed a denial of all that she considered Christian to worship on the "Jewish Sabbath." Not until four long years of poverty and hardship had been the lot of the household did Prudence Bates accept the Sabbath truth. When she did, it was with all her heart. Then for twenty years she was to stand loyally by her husband's side, encouraging him as he traveled far and wide, lifting the banner of the truth.

Chapter Fifteen

The New Plank

JOSEPH BATES was eager to spread the new Sabbath truth. Whenever he met any of his friends, he spoke to them about their duty to keep the fourth commandment by observing the Sabbath.

But if the matter of the Sabbath was clear in his mind, he was still perplexed about something else. Why had Jesus failed to come to earth on October 22, 1844? What mistake had the Advent leaders made in interpreting the prophecy of Daniel 8: 14? One day he received another paper through the mail. It carried the title of *The Day Dawn* and had been issued by Hiram Edson and Dr. Franklin B. Hahn, Adventists living at Port Gibson in central New York. As he read, Bates found his perplexities disappearing. It offered a satisfying solution to his problem. To understand the experience behind this issue of *The Day Dawn*, we must go back to the morning after the great disappointment.

Hiram Edson was one of many thousands who had wept and mourned all night after the sad day when Jesus did not come. As that night had worn on, he and his friends had talked among themselves—questioning, wondering.

"Is there to be no return of Jesus?"

"Is the Bible then false?"

"Shall we never see the golden city, the home of the redeemed, or walk in that country whose inhabitants will not say, 'I am sick'?"

"Not so, brethren," said Hiram Edson. "There is a God and He will hear us. Let us go and implore Him for further light on this matter."

So the brethren went out to the barn, where, on the granary floor, they

89

knelt and prayed; then they returned to the house. After breakfast Edson suggested to a friend that they go over to the home of some other believers to comfort them. As they were taking a short cut through a cornfield, it suddenly seemed to Hiram Edson that a hand gripped his shoulder and a voice spoke, clearly and distinctly, "The sanctuary to be cleansed is in heaven."

Standing there in that cornfield, he seemed to be able to . look up into heaven itself and see the sanctuary with Jesus ministering in the most holy place. His companion had gone on and come to the next fence before realizing that Edson had tarried behind, so he called out:

"Brother Edson, what are you stopping for?"

Brother Edson called back, "God is answering our morning prayer." Hastening, he came up with his friend and began telling him what he had seen and heard).

"My mind," he said, "is carried to the tenth and eleventh chapters of Revelation, where John was told to take a little book from the angel's hand and eat it. It tasted like honey in his mouth, but when he had eaten it, it was as bitter as gall. That is our experience, brother. Was it not sweet to believe that Jesus was coming yesterday? But now it is bitter, very bitter. The sanctuary I saw is in heaven, and Jesus entered yesterday upon His work of cleansing it."

Together they hastened on to talk these points over with their fellow believers. During the next few weeks Edson, Dr. Hahn, and O. R. L. Crozier studied all about the sanctuary built by Moses in the wilderness, patterned after the great sanctuary in heaven, where Jesus is now ministering. Edson and Dr. Hahn were so thrilled by their discovery that they wrote it out and published it in a paper called *The Day Dawn* and sent copies to other Adventists. It explained why Jesus had not come to earth in 1844; how instead He had entered into the most holy place in the heavenly sanctuary to start the work of judgment by examining the records in heaven. One copy of *The Day Dawn* went to James White in Maine and one to Joseph Bates in Fairhaven.

Hiram Edson's heart thrilled when he began to receive replies from those who read this paper, agreeing with what he had written. Both White and Bates replied, "You have the truth," and expressed a strong desire to meet and talk with Edson. As a result of this encouragement, he sent out an invitation for as many of the Advent leaders as possible to come to his home, there to hold a conference. James White could not come, but Joseph Bates was there. He had a secret reason for wanting to attend. He knew that while Edson had given him some very important light, he in turn had new truth for Edson.

So after the brethren had gone over the teaching of the Bible concerning the sanctuary and its cleansing and found themselves in complete agreement, Bates presented the importance of keeping the seventh day as the Sabbath. Hiram Edson had already heard of this truth, but so far he had made no decision. As Joseph Bates now presented the matter in his usual clear fashion, Edson determined to obey.

"It's the truth," he declared, "and I am going to keep the Sabbath."

"So am I," added Dr. Hahn. But Crozier was not so sure.

"Better go slowly, brethren. We don't want to step on any plank until we know whether it will hold us up."

"I have tested this plank already," replied Edson, "and I know it will hold."

Thus the number of Sabbathkeepers increased. Rejoicing in the success of the conference, Joseph Bates returned to Fairhaven.

Chapter Sixteen

The Lord Will Provide

DURING the winter following his visit to Hiram Edson, Joseph Bates continued to think and plan how he could get the wonderful Sabbath truth before the world. He wrote regularly to the Sabbathkeepers in Washington, New Hampshire, and to Edson out in New York State. He visited in the homes of his friends and neighbors, talking with them about the Sabbath, finding some who accepted and others who rejected his message.

Elder Bates had shown his faith in the 1844 message by his works. When October 22 arrived, his fortune had been spent in supporting the cause. He had not revealed the actual state of his finances to his wife, not wishing to worry her sooner than necessary.

Joseph Bates never let a shortage of means stand in his way when duty called. He was a man with great faith in his heavenly Father and frequently showed that faith by his actions. One time he felt impressed to attend a conference of workers being held in Connecticut, but had no money with which to pay his fare. Without a cent in his pockets, he calmly boarded the train, where he sat praying that the Lord would in some way provide in this emergency before the conductor arrived asking for his fare. Feeling a hand on his shoulder, he looked up to see a perfect stranger, who handed him five dollars. They soon parted, and Bates went on his way rejoicing.

One morning as he sat in his study, he felt impressed that the Lord wanted him to write and print a pamphlet setting forth the truth concerning the Sabbath and send it out to the many places where he could not go in person. When Joseph Bates received an impression, he never wasted any time before carrying it out. He brought out his Bible and concordance and before long was busy preparing a rough draft of his subject.

As he sat busily writing, the door opened.

"Joseph," his wife said, "I am sorry to trouble you, but I find I haven't enough flour to finish the baking."

"How much flour do you need?" Joseph asked. "Oh, about four pounds, I suppose," was her reply.

"Very well. I will get it for you." She returned to the kitchen, and Joseph arose and walked to the nearest store, where he purchased with his last coin four pounds of flour and a few other articles he knew were also needed. Returning to the house, he deposited them in the kitchen and went back to his study.

Perhaps Mrs. Bates was outside when he returned, but it was not many minutes before she again stood before his desk, holding the flour in her hand.

"Joseph," she said, holding out the flour, "where did this flour come from?"

"From the store. I went and bought it. Didn't you say you needed four pounds?"

Mrs. Bates looked astonished. "Do you mean to tell me that you, Captain Bates, a man who has sailed vessels out of New Bedford to all parts of the world—that you have gone out and bought *four* pounds of flour?"

"Yes, wife," he replied. "And I might as well tell you that for that flour I paid out the last cent I have."

This was shocking news to Mrs. Bates. She knew how liberal he had always been in supporting the Advent cause, but to suddenly realize that they were penniless filled her with dismay. Lifting her apron to her face, she wept.

"Whatever is going to become of us?" she sobbed. "What are you going to do?"

"I am going to write a book," he replied, "and circulate it and spread this Sabbath truth before the world."

"Yes," replied his wife, "but what are we going to live on?"

"Prudence, you know the Lord will provide," replied her husband in his calm, cheerful manner.

"Yes, that's what you always say, 'The Lord will provide.'" Weeping bitterly, she left the room.

Bates returned to his work, but somehow he found it difficult to concentrate. After a few minutes he felt impressed that a letter awaited him at the post office. Leaving his work, he went down to find out whether there was anything for him. After a greeting, the postmaster told him immediately that there was a letter for him sent postage collect. Bates had to admit that he did not have the necessary money for the postage, but the postmaster pushed the letter toward him with the assurance:

'That's all right, Captain Bates. Take it and pay me some other time." But Bates had a deep abhorrence of debt and declined to take the letter until he could pay for it.

"I have a feeling that there may be money in this letter for me," he told the postmaster. "Will you please open it? If there is no money, I will not take it. If there is, you may deduct the required postage and give me the balance with the letter."

The man agreed and on opening the letter found it contained ten dollars. Under the terms agreed upon, Bates received the letter and his cash balance.

Standing in the post office, Elder Bates read the letter which came from a brother in New Jersey. Somehow he had felt impressed that Bates was in need, so he was sending ten dollars.

"Father, I thank Thee," murmured Joseph Bates.

Thrusting the letter into his pocket, he went to the store, where he bought a barrel of flour as well as quantities of potatoes, sugar, salt, oil, and other provisions. He gave instructions to the drayman to leave the things on the porch of his home, which was well known in Fairhaven. He warned the drayman at the same time that the lady of the house might try to refuse them, but to leave them anyway.

Proceeding across the bridge to the printer, Bates made arrangements to have a thousand copies of his forthcoming pamphlet printed, promising to pay before taking delivery. Then he returned home and quietly slipped into his study. With an untroubled mind he turned back to his writing.

For the third time that morning the door opened and his wife stood before him.

"Joseph," she exclaimed, and it was evident that she was much excited about something, "wherever did those provisions come from which the drayman left on our porch? I told him that they weren't ours, that we had no money to buy such things!"

"Didn't I tell you that the Lord would provide?" Joseph replied, with a quiet smile.

"Yes, the Lord will provide. I would like to know how many times you have said that. But these things didn't fall down from heaven."

Joseph took the letter from his pocket and handed it to his wife.

"Read that, and you will understand."

Obeying, she then went to her room, where, with weeping, she confessed her lack of faith and sought forgiveness.

In the month of August, 1846, Bates was informed that he might take delivery of his pamphlet, "The Seventh Day Sabbath, a Perpetual Sign," at the printers. He had paid part of the cost as money had come to him, but quite a balance was still due. He asked the Lord to send it to him soon.

During all of those trying months H. S. Gurney had remained one of the closest friends of Elder Bates. He entered into all his plans, encouraging him in every way he could. He was a faithful layman, plying his trade as a blacksmith.

Back in the winter of 1843 Gurney had been working for a large firm in New Bedford. When he was invited to accompany Bates on his evangelistic trip into the South, Gurney had accepted, and going to his employer, he had handed in his resignation. It so happened that the company owed him one hundred dollars. When he tried to collect, the owner told him that his leaving so abruptly would do a hundred dollars' worth of damage to the business and that under the circumstances he would pay nothing. Although Gurney's friends told him he had a clear case, he refused to take the matter to court.

Now three years later, in the very month of August when Bates was waiting for money to pay the printer for his pamphlets, Gurney happened one day to meet his old employer on the street. Stopping the surprised blacksmith, he said with a rather embarrassed look:

"See here, Gurney, you know I really do owe you that hundred dollars, and I am going to pay you now. I am ashamed of the way I treated you." With that he handed the astonished Mr. Gurney one hundred dollars.

"This is the Lord's doing," said Gurney to himself. "I am going to pay for those pamphlets for Elder Bates." Going immediately to the printer, he paid the balance due.

Thus it came about that when Bates went a few days later to explain why he had not taken delivery of his pamphlets, the printer told him that they were all paid for. The completed job was placed in his hands. "But who paid for them?" asked Elder Bates in astonishment. "I cannot tell," replied the printer. "He was a complete stranger to me."

To the day of his death Joseph Bates never knew who had paid that account for him. But he did see in it the gracious hand of his heavenly Father.

Chapter Seventeen

A Doubting Thomas

"PREPARE the guest room, dear," said Elder Joseph Bates to his wife one morning in early 1846 as he stepped into the kitchen, an open letter in his hand.

"Why, who is coming?" was her natural response.

"Ellen Harmon and her sister from Maine. Elder White is coming also."

"Isn't Ellen the one who you said claims to have visions from God?"

"That's right. They are coming to visit the Advent believers in New Bedford and Fairhaven."

"But didn't you say that you have no faith in her visions?"

"Yes, Prudy, and I still don't know what to think about it. I shall now be able to talk with her more fully." As soon as the visitors arrived, a number of meetings were arranged during which Elder White spoke words of exhortation, and Ellen Harmon told of the things she had been shown in vision. To many who listened strong conviction came that this was a message from heaven. Elder Bates, though, found all the old doubts still lingering in his mind.

Rising in the meeting, he said to all those present:

"I am a doubting Thomas. I do not believe in visions. If I could believe that the testimony the sister has related tonight was indeed the voice of God to us, I would be the happiest man alive. I believe the speaker to be sincere, but cannot explain in regard to her being shown the wonderful things she has related to us."

If Joseph Bates was not prepared to accept her messages as from Heaven, neither were the visitors prepared to accept his doctrine on the duty of Christians to keep the seventh-day Sabbath. Ellen Harmon felt that Elder Bates made a mistake in emphasizing the Sabbath Commandment more than the other nine.

Patiently and kindly Elder Bates answered the objections raised as best he could. In mid-August Elder White was again in New Bedford and Fairhaven. This was just a few days before he and Ellen Harmon were to be married in Portland, Maine. It was this month that Elder Bates's pamphlet on the Sabbath truth was printed, and James White accepted one of the pamphlets, promising that he and Ellen would give it careful study. Elder and Mrs. White, soon after their marriage on August 30, were both convinced of the Sabbath and began to keep it.

Elder Bates on his part was determined to settle in his own mind whether the messages of Ellen White were from Heaven. He made a trip to Maine and talked with her father and mother, thus being assured that Ellen had come from a sincere Christian family. He visited with her friends and neighbors, who freely testified to the pure and virtuous life she had always led. They pointed out how she had brought hope, joy, love, and harmony into the midst of the Advent believers.

In November, 1846, at a meeting in Topsham, Maine, Joseph Bates was present when Mrs. White was taken off in vision. For the first time she was given a view of some of the planets and of the starry heavens. While in vision, she graphically described what she was seeing, especially thrilling the hearts of her listeners as she spoke of the great open space in the constellation of Orion. During his years at sea Bates had made a special study of astronomy, and as he listened, his heart was mightily stirred. He arose and exclaimed, "Oh, how I wish Lord William Rosse were here!"

"Who is Lord William Rosse?" asked James White.

"He is the great English astronomer who made a deep study of Orion and has written so much about it. But this description surpasses anything ever written by him."

After her vision Joseph Bates took the opportunity to speak with Mrs. White.

"When did you study astronomy, Mrs. White?" he asked.

"To my knowledge," she replied, "I have never opened an astronomy book in my life."

"That settles it," declared Elder Bates, his face beaming. "I thank God for the opportunity I have had with others here tonight to witness these things."

Never again did the former "doubting Thomas" have the slightest question in his mind that through Ellen G. White, the testimony of Jesus, the Spirit of prophecy, spoke to the remnant church.

Having settled the matter in his own mind, Elder Bates was now eager to associate further with Elder and Mrs. White. It was arranged that he should travel with them for a while as they went from place to place, confirming the faith of the believers and presenting the truth of the Sabbath to those who had not yet heard it.

To make one journey, a two-seated market wagon drawn by a colt was placed at their disposal. Unfortunately, the colt was known to be bad-tempered, but just how vicious the Whites and Elder Bates did not fully know. They were warned that if any line or hand touched his flanks, he would kick out savagely, and the reins had to be held firmly to prevent him from running away. This same colt had already killed two men in a runaway accident, but of this the Whites knew nothing.

As they traveled, Elder and Mrs. White occupied the front seat while Bates and Israel Damon sat behind. As they rode along, the Spirit of God came upon Mrs. White in mighty power. Giving expression in a beautiful voice, she exclaimed, "Glory! Glory! Glory!" And she was taken off in vision. At the same instant the colt stopped of its own accord. Mrs. White then stood up. Her eyes were open. She placed her hand on the flank of the colt, and stepped from the wagon onto the ground. Greatly alarmed, Elder Bates called out:

"The colt will kick that woman to death!"

"The Lord has the colt in charge now; I do not wish to interfere," replied Elder White.

Mrs. White climbed to the green grassy bank by the side of the road where she walked up and down for several minutes. During the entire time the colt stood perfectly still.

"Watch," said Elder White, gently touching the horse with the end of the whip. The colt gave not the slightest indication that anything had happened. Elder White struck him harder, but he stood perfectly still.

After a time Mrs. White returned to the wagon, placed her hand again on the flank of the colt, climbed in, and resumed her seat. At the same instant she drew her first deep breath, indicating that the vision was over. Only then did the colt, without a word from the driver, begin to trot along the road. This experience strongly impressed Elder Bates, deepening his conviction that the visions were from Heaven.

Chapter Eighteen

Ask Elder Bates

JOSEPH BATES sat in his study reading a letter he had just received. It contained an invitation from Elder James White for him to attend a conference of Sabbath keepers in the town of Volney in western New York.

"I think I will go," he said to himself. "We need to get together and try to bring some unity into our teachings. He says here that he will be in New York City on the thirteenth, and if I can meet him, we can travel on together."

Having made his decision, Bates lost no time putting it into effect. Hunting up his good friend Gurney, he invited him to go also, and was happy when that worthy man accepted. On the day appointed, therefore, both were happily welcomed in New York City, from whence they traveled in a group to the Volney meeting. Here they found about thirty-five believers gathered together. They had no church building, and there was no house with a room sufficiently large for them, so they met in David Arnold's barn.

As Elder Bates had feared, when the brethren began to talk together, they found many different ideas and beliefs being held by different ones. In fact, it seemed difficult to find two who were in complete agreement on any subject.

"Let us celebrate the Lord's Supper," Elder White suggested. "That is one service, at least, in which we can all unite and show brotherly love one for another."

But even in this he was mistaken. As they surrounded the Lord's table, David Arnold arose and declared that he had no confidence in what they were about to do.

"The Lord's Supper," he protested, "is a continuation of the Jewish Passover which was held once a year. It is wrong to hold it more often."

"Not so, brother," quickly replied Elder White. "The first disciples held this service very frequently as we can read in the Book of Acts." So he continued with the service, but the sweet spirit seemed to be missing.

Watching these signs of discord, Ellen White experienced great sorrow of heart. So great was the burden that she fainted, and some thought she was dying. Around her bedside gathered Elders White and Bates with Brethren Chamberlain, Gurney, and Hiram Edson. Most earnestly did they pray for her recovery, and their prayers were answered. The power of God came into the room, and she was taken off in vision, which lasted for a long time. In this vision she was shown the errors of many of the brethren present at the conference.

On emerging from this vision, she spoke freely to those present, pointing out their mistakes, and urging all to come into line and stand on the platform of truth. The ones who had been in error arose, renouncing their mistakes. The sweet influence of heaven came into their midst, and they united in praising God for sending them light in the midst of their perplexity.

From Volney they traveled to Port Gibson, entering the hospitable home of Hiram Edson, where another conference was held for the believers in that area, again in a barn. One of the questions about which there had been much discussion was in regard to the Sabbath.

When the conference had ended, Elder and Mrs. White and Elder Bates left for New York City, where they hoped to spend the following Sabbath. The three of them went together to the side of the Erie Canal to wait for the packet. As it approached, they could see that it was not going to stop for them. So Elder White picked up his little wife, gave a mighty spring, and landed safely on the deck.

Elder Bates was not so fortunate. As the boat drew near, he was holding the fare (a dollar bill) in one hand and his purse in the other. Holding out the money to the captain as he moved past, Bates shouted, "Here, take your pay!" Apparently the captain did not hear, for he paid no attention.

Elder Bates then tried to imitate Elder White by springing on board. Perhaps the packet was now farther from the pier, for in spite of making a strong jump, his foot struck on the edge of the boat, and he fell backward into the canal. A gasp went up from the people standing and watching on deck. Coming to the surface, Bates began to tread water vigorously, still holding the dollar bill in one hand and his pocketbook in the other. The canal boat slowed down and stopped. Working his way toward the boat, Bates lost his hat. In trying to recover it, he dropped the dollar bill, but held on to his pocketbook.

Slowly he drew near the packet, where eager hands reached down and pulled him on board. What a sight he was, with water dripping from his hair, off his clothes, and running out of his shoes! Fortunately it was a warm summer day, and the three travelers sat together on deck in the sunshine until the boat reached Centerport, the home of Brother Harris. Here they left the packet and stayed for a day, thus giving Brother Bates a chance to get his clothes pressed.

Because of this delay, they had to give up their plan of getting to New York before Sabbath. On Friday afternoon they rode up in a hired carriage to the door of Brother Ira Abbey's home in Brookfield. Would they be able to spend the Sabbath day with this family?

Elder White went to the door and knocked. Mrs. Abbey opened it, and he introduced himself.

"Elder White!" she exclaimed. "I am so glad to see you. Come in."

"There are three more of our party still in the carriage," he admitted. "I thought if we all came in together, we might frighten you."

"I am never frightened by Christians," was her cheerful reply.

Elder White then returned to the carriage, and the rest of the party went up to the house, where he introduced them to Sister Abbey.

"Can this be Brother Bates who wrote that hewing book on the Sabbath?" she asked, grasping his hand. "And come to see us? I am not worthy to have you come under my roof."

In a few minutes Brother Abbey came in from the field where he had been working, and they spent a most enjoyable Sabbath together.

Shortly after leaving here the party separated, the Whites going their way, and Bates and Gurney directing their steps once again toward Fairhaven. The trip had proved a great blessing to Elder Bates, and he returned home to make new plans for spreading the wonderful message, which gripped his heart more firmly every day.

Chapter Nineteen

In Search of Gold

*J*OSEPH, must you go again so soon?"

Prudence stood in the bedroom doorway and watched as her husband carefully packed his bag. Only ten days ago he had returned after an absence of six months, spent in traveling through every New England state, stopping at scores of towns and villages. The roaming sailor of early youth had now become a land rover, going far and near, ever carrying with him the news of a soon-coming Saviour, and calling attention to the duty of all men to keep the seventh day as the Sabbath of the Lord.

Joseph Bates paused in his work and said with a gentle smile, "Yes, dear, I expect to take the cars tomorrow."

"And where are you going this time?" continued his wife.

"I expect to go west, to visit places I have never seen be fore," he replied.

"No! Joseph, no!" Prudence objected. "I cannot bear to have you go so far away. It will take you months just to reach there, and when will I hear from you again?"

Joseph understood what his wife meant and smiled again.

"No, Prudy, I didn't mean I was going to California. I am only planning to visit Ohio, Indiana, Michigan, and perhaps then go over into Canada. You know that many of the scattered sheep have settled in those parts, and I wish to take the Sabbath truth to them."

The year was 1849, and the United States was gripped by the greatest gold fever in its history. Tens of thousands of men had left their homes and work in the East to take the overland trail for California, the land of gold. It was a long and dangerous journey, whether made by ship around Cape Horn or by overland wagons across the plains and through the Rocky Mountains.

"Then you will be traveling by train all the way?" questioned Prudence.

"That is right. The railway reaches into all of the states I intend visiting. I have carried this blessed truth into nearly every part of New England. How can I rest easily when I know that in those western states are poor scattered believers who have not heard the good news? I must go to instruct and strengthen them."

Only a short time before, in this same year, Prudence had decided that her husband was right after all and had begun to keep the seventh day as the Sabbath, much to the joy of her husband. This helped to reconcile her somewhat to Joseph's proposed journey.

The following day Elder Bates took the train for New York, where he changed cars and continued his journey over the Allegheny Mountains down into the Ohio Valley, where he began his work. Systematically he then went from town to town, never stopping more than a few days in any one place, ever seeking out the Adventists, as those who had looked for Jesus to come in 1844 were still called.

Whenever he found these Adventists, whether they were few or many, he met with them. They usually invited this stranger to speak to them; so hanging up his charts, he brought them the new message, calling on them to worship God on His holy Sabbath day. Many were the hard hearts he met, and often he was ridiculed and laughed at, but Joseph Bates was not easily discouraged. If only he could find a few who would listen, accept, and obey, he was satisfied.

Leaving Ohio, Bates went into Indiana and was holding meetings in South Bend when one night he had an impressive dream. He seemed to be traveling by stage, going northeast to a village, the name of which was not revealed to him. He awoke with the impression that he should go there, as in that place the Lord had precious souls who would hear and accept the truth.

Northeast would take him into Michigan, at that time a young state, but already boasting a population of nearly half a million. Elder Bates decided to go immediately, although he was unsure of his destination. Feeling confident that he would recognize the town when he saw it, he took the stage. At every town where they stopped, Bates would alight, look around, and after deciding that this was not the place he sought, would pay the fare and proceed to the next town. The driver no doubt thought him slightly mad, but made no objection so long as he received the necessary fare.

The coach came to the town of Jackson. One quick glance and Joseph Bates recognized this as the place he had seen in his dream. With his small bag he left the coach and walked up the main street. Finding a boarding house, he asked the owner:

"Are there any Adventists living in this town?"

"Yes, about twenty meet here every Sunday."

These Adventists were still looking for the return of Jesus, but as yet had heard nothing about the Sabbath.

Proceeding up the street, Bates came to the open door of a shop. Here Dan Palmer, a blacksmith, was busy at his forge and anvil, putting a shoe on a horse. Elder Bates stepped into the shop, gave his name, hung his chart on a convenient nail, and proceeded to talk about the truths he loved so well. At first Palmer paid little attention to what was being said, but little by little the message began to sink in, and he would pause and listen to a few sentences. The pauses became longer and longer until finally Palmer stopped work altogether, stepped up to Bates, and thrusting out his horny hand said in a friendly way:

"Brother—what did you say your name was?—Bates, you have the truth!" He immediately invited Bates to meet with the little group the following Sunday. Elder Bates was happy to accept. At this meeting he presented the Sabbath truth in such a convincing way that the entire company accepted it. Dan Palmer was a man of means and was used by God in later years to help greatly in building up the work, not only in Jackson, but in other parts of Michigan as well. On that same Sunday afternoon following the meeting, Palmer drove Elder Bates out into the country to see a farmer friend of his, Cyrenius Smith, who had not been at the meeting. A short visit and Smith and his entire family accepted the truth.

Thus Bates continued his work, ever traveling while the weeks and months passed by. As winter came on, he decided to return home to his family. He also wished to get in touch with Elder and Mrs. White and tell them of the promising field for spreading the message he had found in the West. The train took

Advancing up the street, Bates came to the open door of a shop. Stepping in, he gave his name, hung his chart on a convenient-nail, and proceeded to talk about the truths he loved so well.

him back once more to Fairhaven, where he found his wife, as always, very happy to see him. They had many things to talk over, each relating the various happenings that had taken place at home and abroad.

During the years which followed, as he traveled from place to place, Elder Bates wrote regular letters to Elder White telling of his experiences, and these letters were printed in *The Review and Herald*. The paper was then appearing once a fortnight, and there was scarcely an issue which did not carry a letter or an article from this roving pioneer missionary. His heart rejoiced as he read it and saw how the influence of the little band of Sabbath keepers was spreading. They were not as yet called Seventh-day Adventists. That name was not to be adopted for another ten years.

Chapter Twenty

I Have Seen You Before

ELDER BATES, I cannot tell you how happy I am that you came to West Wilton at this time," said Mrs. Smith, a woman who lived in a small town in New Hampshire.

She had been a firm believer in the first Advent message as preached by William Miller, and her son and daughter, Uriah and Annie, had believed with her. Following the disappointment, the two children began to lose the faith they had once so firmly held. They were no longer sure that Jesus was soon coming, at least in their lifetime. Should they not make preparation for life-work in this world?

They talked the matter over with their mother, in whom they had the utmost confidence. After much discussion both children had decided to take a teaching course, and when Elder Bates came to West Wilton, they were away attending their respective schools. When the Sabbath had been presented to the little company of Adventists in town, Mrs. Smith gladly accepted it. She immediately thought of her children and longed to tell them all about her new faith.

"Elder Bates, won't you pray with me for their conversion?" she asked the kindly minister. "I am so troubled about them. They are good children, but the attractions of the world are so strong. Oh, if only they could see and accept this wonderful truth about the Sabbath, I would be so happy."

"Where are your son and daughter, Sister Smith?"

"Uriah is attending Phillips' Academy in Exeter, and Annie is in her final year at a seminary in Charlestown, Massachusetts. Both of them have been invited to teach next year at the same academy and have been promised a thousand dollars a year with room and board."

"A thousand dollars!" exclaimed Elder Bates. "That is a very attractive offer to young people these days. Now I am going to be holding some meetings in Somerville, at the home of Paul Folsom, not far from the school which Annie is attending. Why don't you write and invite her to attend my meetings? I should be there to hold the first one next Sabbath."

"I will do it, Elder Bates. God bless you. I believe the Lord will touch Annie's heart and lead her aright."

Together the minister and the burdened mother then knelt and poured out their prayers in behalf of the two young people.

Elder Bates then went on to Somerville, where he prepared to hold his first service. That Friday night he had a remarkable dream. He seemed to be in the room where his meeting was to be held. Just as they were singing the last stanza of the opening hymn, a young lady, whom somehow he knew to be Annie Smith, came in and took the only vacant chair near the door. He had planned to speak on another subject, but on seeing her, he quoted the text, "Unto two thousand and three hundred days; then shall the sanctuary be cleansed." He then proceeded to preach about the sanctuary service and the Sabbath.

That same Friday Annie had received a letter from her mother, urging her to attend the meeting Elder Bates would be holding the next day.

"I would much rather go with you," she told a friend with whom she had made other plans for that Saturday, "but mother seems so eager for me to go and hear what Elder Bates has to say. I couldn't bear to write and tell her I didn't have time, when I really do. You understand, don't you?" Her friend nodded.

"Yes, just to please mother I will go," said Annie to herself. "After all, it's a holiday."

Elder Bates was not the only one who had a striking dream that Friday night. Annie had one also. She thought she was attending a meeting in a large room. They were singing the last stanza of the opening hymn when she entered late and took the only vacant chair by the door. The speaker, whom she had never seen before, spoke from a text in Daniel about the cleansing of the sanctuary. When she awoke in the morning, she pondered her dream. She knew she would recognize the speaker if she saw him.

Both dreams were fulfilled. Elder Bates had really intended speaking on another topic, but changed his mind when the young lady, whom he instantly knew must be Annie Smith, entered the room and took the only vacant chair during the singing of the hymn. She had lost her way while coming, otherwise she would have been in plenty of time, having started early.

"Unto two thousand and three hundred days; then shall the sanctuary be cleansed," Elder Bates read out in a clear, ringing voice.

Annie sank back in her chair. That was the very text, this was the room, and there was the speaker she had seen in her dream. Her heart was naturally prepared to accept the truths she heard. At the close of the meeting, having presented the truth of the third angel's message and the Sabbath, Elder Bates made his way to Annie. Taking the hand which she put out to greet him, Elder Bates said with a broad smile on his kindly face:

"I believe this is Sister Smith's daughter. I never saw you before, but your countenance looks familiar. I dreamed of seeing you last night."

"Oh, Elder Bates," Annie replied fervently, "I dreamed of seeing you here, and I believe every word you spoke is the truth."

"Your mother will surely rejoice to hear that," replied the minister.

So it came about that a few weeks later, in that summer of 1851, Annie packed her trunk and returned home to stay with her mother until she knew what the Lord wanted her to do. Together mother and daughter prayed for the conversion of Uriah. On learning of the cares of Elder and Mrs. White in publishing the *Review and Herald* at Saratoga Springs, New York, she felt impressed to join them and assist in publishing the message.

The next year Uriah was persuaded to attend a general meeting of believers in Washington, New Hampshire, and before the end of 1852 he also had decided to cast in his lot with the peculiar group of people keeping the seventh day of the week instead of the first. At the same time he was fired with determination to give his life spreading the truth which seemed so wonderful to him.

Cabin Boy

In March, 1853, he joined the little group connected with the publishing work, now located in Rochester, New York.

The future, of course, was veiled from the sight of these two young people. Would Annie have gone had she known that ere three short years had passed, she would be called upon to lay down her life, a victim of the terrible scourge tuberculosis? From what we know of Annie Smith we may be sure this would have made no difference. Uriah's services with the *Review and Herald* office, as it came to be known, were to stretch on and on for fifty long, fruitful years.

Annie never forgot the wonderful way in which God had used Joseph Bates to bring the message to her. She always respected him as a minister and loved him as a father.

At this time Elder Bates was nearly sixty years of age. He was a warrior, tried and true. As long as God gave him strength, he would continue to labor in His vineyard. His face might be furrowed with anxiety and perplexity at times, but his step was still vigorous, and no words of discouragement ever fell from his lips. It was this warrior whom Annie described in the first stanza of a beautiful poem she wrote for *The Advent Review and Sabbath Herald*, later to be set to music and sung by Adventists around the world. It is entitled "I Saw One Weary" and may be found in the Church Hymnal, No. 371.

> "I saw one weary, sad, and torn,
> With eager steps press on the way,
> Who long the hallowed cross had borne,
> Still waiting for the promised day;
> While many a line of grief and care,
> Upon his brow was furrowed there;
> I asked what buoyed his spirits up,
> 'O this!' said he—'the blessed hope.'"

Chapter Twenty-One

Braving the
Winter Snows

TWO years slipped by after the return of Joseph Bates from his first visit to Michigan. They were years of busy activity in the New England States. Like the Apostle Paul of old, Bates longed to see again the faces of his converts and to know if they were standing firmly in the truth he had made known to them. But there was another region which seemed to call to him, "Come over and help us," and that was the part of Canada lying just north of Lake Ontario. In those days it was called Canada West, although now it is the province of Ontario. Bates knew that in those settlements, often far back in the woods, there were many precious souls who might never come in contact with the city workers.

Although his wife, as usual, protested when he suggested making another long journey, he steadfastly went ahead with his plans.

"But, Joseph," she objected, "you should not make these long journeys now. How do you expect to travel in that lonely country?"

"I shall have to cover most of it on foot, I suppose," he answered cheerfully.

"But why go in winter, when the roads will be blocked by snow?" she persisted.

"Because I could not rest at home knowing there were souls perishing for want of the truth I can bring them."

"Joseph, if you are going to make this journey on foot, then I am sure you should not try to make it now. Remember, you will soon be sixty, and it is time for you to begin slowing down."

"Prudy, dear," he replied, "I feel as well and strong today as I did twenty years ago. God has blessed me with splendid health, especially since I have known how to take care of it. You know it has been a long time since I suffered from sickness of any kind."

"Will you visit Michigan before you return home?"

"Yes, my present plan will take me into that state once more before I finish this tour. God sparing my life, I should be in Jackson again sometime next spring."

"At least you should choose someone to go with you, so in case of need you would have a helper."

"That sounds like a good suggestion. I will think about it, and perhaps I can find someone willing to go with me."

As a result, Joseph Bates wrote to Hiram Edson, his old friend still living in western New York, and invited him to share in the proposed journey into Canada West. Edson replied that he would gladly join Elder Bates and suggested a time and place where they could meet. So at the appointed time the two dauntless warriors met at Auburn, New York, and plunged together into the Canadian wilderness. Perhaps you would like to hear Joseph Bates' description of the journey, just as he wrote it in a letter to Elder James White, more than a century ago, for *The Review and Herald*. It was written from Toronto in January, 1852, as the two brethren were nearing the end of their Canadian journey.

"Dear Brother White:

"Since I started in October last on my Western tour, I have visited many places in western New York. I held meetings in several places with our Sabbathkeeping brethren, who are loving the present truth more and more. In many places we found the brethren in deep trials; but praying, and perseverance in the straight truths that the little flock now see in their pathway soon triumphed over the enemy, and our hearts were made glad and healed by the precious saving truths of the third angel's message.

"Brother Edson met me at Auburn, New York. We crossed the St. Lawrence for Canada West, the last week in November, and have been working our way to the West, along the south shore of Lake Ontario, and wherever we have learned that there were scattered sheep in the back settlements north of us, we have waded through the deep snow from two to forty miles to find them, and give the present truth; so that in five weeks we have traveled hundreds of miles, and gained on the direct road westward one hundred and eighty miles. We expect to close our labors here by the fifth, and then go north again to Lake Cincoe, where we learn there are some of the scattered flock. From thence it is probable we shall pass on the same course westward to the borders of Lake Huron and Erie. When we have finished our labors between these seas, we expect to return towards Rochester, New York.

"The first twenty days of our journey we were much tried with the deep snow, and tedious cold weather, and with but few exceptions, cold and impenetrable hearts. The truth was no food for them. Since that time the scene has changed and the truth begun to take effect, and some we trust are now searching for the truth. At Mariposa and Scewgog Lakes, thirty and forty miles in the back settlements, and about sixty from here, we found many hungry for the truth. Their minister (Peter Hough), objected to our message, and labored hard to do away with the Sabbath of the Lord our God, and called upon his congregation to decide, concluding that his arguments were clear. About twelve out of twenty enlisted under the banner of the third angel, while but two, I believe, showed a sign in his favor. The rest we left in deep study, saying they would examine the subject.

"In Reach, eight more confessed the whole truth, and three other families admitted the Sabbath to be right. In both of these places they are united in their monthly meetings. Their meetings were appointed for the last Sabbath. They have hopes of their other brethren, because they know them to be honest. These two companies of brethren and sisters seem strong and united, and remind me very much of the Melbourn and Eaton companies in Canada East, that were so prompt and decided to move out on the Lord's side as soon as the truth was presented.

"You will see by the list of names for the paper, and also other names that we send in with those that they are hungering and thirsting for the truth in the

*Whenever Bates and Edson learned that there were scattered believers
in the back settlements, they waded through the deep snow from
two to forty miles to find them and give the present truth.*

last message. We believe that God has precious jewels in Canada West. We have no misgivings about this being the field of our labor for the present. O God, speed the work of gathering the 144,000 here, and all over the world. Amen.

"Your brother,

"Joseph Bates"

Chapter Twenty-Two

The Most Honest Man in Town

THE snow was melting fast on an early day in spring when Joseph Bates and Hiram Edson arrived in Rochester, New York, having finished their strenuous winter march through Canada. Here they spent a pleasant Sabbath with the workers in the home of Elder and Mrs. James White. Elder Bates handed in the names of many new believers scattered through the Canadian back country, who wished in the future to keep in touch with fellow believers through the columns of *The Review and Herald*. Here in Rochester, Bates and Edson parted company, the former turning westward, while Edson returned to his home in Port Gibson.

Two years had passed since Joseph Bates had raised up the little company in Jackson, Michigan. Alighting from the cars, he made his way to the ever-hospitable home of Dan Palmer, the town blacksmith.

"Mighty glad to see you, Elder Bates," said Palmer, thrusting out his hand in friendly greeting. "I have some friends who are studying the truth, and you are just the man to bring them to a decision. I will arrange an early meeting so that they can hear you."

"How is the company, Brother Palmer?"

"Oh, we have been growing since you were here last. Quite a number are ready for examination and baptism, I believe. Several of the young folk have been waiting for your return."

"That's fine," replied Elder Bates. "I shall be happy to meet with these interested ones as soon as possible."

So a time was set for a service to be held in Palmer's spacious parlor, and he sent out word inviting everybody he knew to come. They were specifically told to bring their Bibles and be prepared to ask Elder Bates any questions they had in their minds.

"Above all, I must get word to Merritt Cornell and try to get him to attend," remarked Palmer.

"Who is he?" asked Elder Bates.

"He is a first-day Adventist minister and bitterly opposed to the seventh-day Sabbath. He is a smart young man and has some pretty strong arguments. I know you will have no trouble answering him, but he was almost too much for an unlearned man like me."

Merritt Cornell was a man of action. No sooner did he learn that a man had arrived who claimed he could prove from the Bible that it was the duty of all men to obey the "Jewish" Sabbath, as he called it, and that he was holding a meeting in Dan Palmer's home on a certain afternoon, than the young preacher decided to go into battle. So on the day appointed he and his wife drove up in front of Palmer's door.

"It is too bad that Palmer had to get mixed up on this subject," Cornell remarked to his wife. "I am positive that I can overthrow this seventh-day man, and if Dan sees me do it, we may get him back yet. Have you changed your mind and decided to go in with me?" asked Merritt.

"No, I shall not!" declared Mrs. Cornell decisively. "I have no intention of letting him upset my thinking on that subject."

"You shouldn't be afraid of that when I'm around. However, if you aren't going in, hold the lines while I go in and settle him."

So Angie Cornell was left in the buggy waiting for her husband to return. But the time went by, and after an hour she tied the horse to the hitching post and went in to see what was going on. One after another of his strongest arguments in favor of keeping Sunday had been advanced by the first-day preacher; but his positions had been quietly swept away by Biblical answers made by his opponent. The man he was up against was none other than Joseph Bates, the foremost champion of the Sabbath truth in Adventist ranks at the time. As a last resort, Comell brought forth a tract which sought to show that the law had been abolished at the time of Christ's death on the cross. Since the hour was late, another meeting was appointed for the following day; interest in the subject was keen.

The next morning they met again with Mrs. Comell present, and by the time the four-hour session closed, Elder Bates had succeeded in completely demolishing the arguments presented in the tract. Not only that, but the young man himself was convinced that it was his personal duty to keep the Sabbath.

"Angie," he said, turning to his wife, "this is the truth. I am going to keep the Sabbath."

"But, Merritt," she replied, "what could we do if we were to observe the seventh day? You know that you would be obliged to resign the pastorate which you have been called to fill."

The reply was quick and characteristic: "Angie, if this is the truth, the Lord will open some other way for us, and I will try it."

The Lord had plenty for this young man of only twenty-six years to do. Returning to his home, he won two notable converts to the Sabbath truth within two weeks; the first, a neighbor friend, J. P. Kellogg, and then his father-in-law, Henry Lyon. Both of these men became pillars of the Advent Movement in Michigan. Comell himself was to go on preaching the message for another forty-one years, winning hundreds of converts in all parts of the United States. Had Joseph Bates been able to see into the future, he would have felt that this was one day which had been most profitably spent.

From Jackson, Elder Bates now proposed going into Indiana to visit acquaintances living there. Shortly before his departure, he had another dream. He seemed to be on a vessel going west from Jackson and was told that he must stop and work in Battle Creek. The next morning he put the question to his host.

"Is there a village west of here called Battle Creek?"

"Yes, it is about forty miles up the railroad."

"Do any Adventists live there?"

"Not one that I know of."

"I must go there, as I was shown last night in a dream that it was to be my next place of labor."

Of course, when Bates spoke of Adventists, he was still referring to those who had shared in the great disappointment eight years before and who were now scattered through many of the western states.

The next day he took the early morning mail train, which would get him to Battle Creek about breakfast time. As he neared the station, he wondered how he would begin his work. Then it occurred to him that an honest person would doubtless accept the message he had come to give. It seemed as if a voice spoke to him, bidding him go to the post office and inquire for the most honest man in town.

Alighting from the train, Bates went immediately to the post office, which was just opening. "Can you direct me to the most honest man in this town?" inquired Elder Bates of the rather startled clerk.

"I can give you a direct answer," replied the postmaster. "He is a Christian by the name of Hewitt, living on Van Buren Street, and has the reputation of being the most honest man in these parts. His house is on the right of the street, and there is a little log cabin on the opposite side."

A few minutes later Elder Bates was rapping at the door of the house, which was opened by Mr. Hewitt.

"I have been directed to you," Bates said, "as the most honest man in town. If this is so, I have some important truth to present to you. "

"Come in," Hewitt replied. "We are just sitting down to breakfast. You must eat with us, and then we will listen to you."

While partaking of breakfast, Hewitt was silently sizing up Elder Bates. It did not take him long to see that his visitor was a deeply religious man, so he invited him to conduct family worship, which he did. Then Hewitt quietly said, "Now we will hear what you have to tell us."

Joseph Bates hung up the chart which he carried everywhere. During the morning he explained the Advent Movement, for Hewitt was a Presbyterian and had not experienced the disappointment. Then in the afternoon he outlined the third angel's message and presented the Sabbath. By five o'clock "the most honest man in town" and his wife were convinced that Bates spoke the truth and resolved to keep the next Sabbath. Elder Bates continued visiting in Battle Creek, and it was not long before a small but faithul company were meeting Sabbath by Sabbath in the Hewitt home.

121

Alighting from the train, Bates went immediately to the post office. "Can you direct me to the most honest man in this town?" he inquired of the startled clerk.

The following spring Elder James White visited Battle Creek and met with the little company. "I am much impressed that if you are all faithful, there will yet be quite a company in Battle Creek," he said. Those were prophetic words indeed!

"Homeward bound!" The words and thought were still sweet music to the heart of Joseph Bates as the train clicked off the miles which stretched between Michigan and his Fairhaven home.

"It is a wonderful country, Prudy," he told his wife. "The people are open-hearted and generous. They seem more ready to accept the message than many whom I have visited in these eastern states."

"Are you thinking of moving to Michigan?" inquired his wife, a note of anxiety creeping into her voice. "I have thought of it several times," Joseph replied with conviction.

"You mean after making Fairhaven and New Bedford your home for sixty years you are thinking of transplanting yourself and moving to another state?"

"Yes, I think it may come."

'When will that be?"

"I cannot say now. The Lord will open the way," was the characteristic response of Joseph Bates.

Chapter Twenty-Three

The Dauntless Missionary

WHEN Joseph Bates reached home again in the late summer of 1852, after an absence of nearly nine months, he had recently celebrated his sixtieth birthday.

"Now surely, Joseph, you will be willing to settle down," urged his ever loving and dutiful wife. "May we not look forward to spending the remaining years together which the Lord shall grant us?"

"Prudy, you know I could not do that. So long as there is work to do which I can do, I must answer the call of duty. I know it is hard on you and that at times you find it extremely lonely. After all, there is all eternity which we can enjoy together. Only a few more years and the night cometh when no man can work."

"But, Joseph, you are sixty years old. You owe it to yourself to lighten up the strenuous life you are leading."

"Wife, I feel well, very well indeed. I cannot remain inactive while my brethren are carrying such heavy burdens. Do you remember what Elder White said not long ago when someone suggested he take a rest?"

"No, what did he say?"

" 'Better to wear out than to rust out,' and I think that is a pretty good motto."

There was to be no slackening in the work of Joseph Bates for many years to come. During the next six years he continued his constant traveling, using his Fairhaven home as port of call.

It would not be possible even to list all the places where he held meetings during those years. Faithfully he wrote to Elder White concerning his varied activities, letters which continued to appear regularly in *The Review and Herald*. Almost every letter was dated from a different town, indicating how ceaselessly he was on the move. By 1855 his reports were going regularly every fortnight to two or three thousand Adventist homes.

Suppose we follow him on some of those trips to see what manner of man he was and how he went about the work he frequently referred to as searching for the "lost sheep." Between the second of February and the eleventh of March, 1853, in company with Hiram Edson, he visited some twenty places, holding meetings. In one town he was conducting a service in the parlor of a certain Brother Ashley, where a newly married couple sat before him, the young husband not even a Christian. Elder Bates sent the truth home to that young man's heart with power and conviction. Seeing that he was deeply troubled, Elder Bates spoke directly to him at the close of the meeting. "What are you going to do with this truth that you have heard today?"

"I am going to keep the Sabbath," the young man replied emphatically. Elder Bates turned his eyes on the young wife. "I shall do so also," she replied with equal conviction.

Not all his experiences ended as happily as this. In Galesburgh, Michigan, he was preaching in a house when a man jumped up, saying he had kept the Sabbath only to please others, but he himself knew that the commandments were all abolished. As the man then poured out a perfect tirade such as Bates had never heard before, he turned to the owner of the home in which he was holding the service.

"I shall not be able to preach this evening if this brawler is allowed to carry on in this fashion."

Since no assurance was given, Elder Bates left. He spent the evening walking eight miles to call on some believers whom he heard were wavering in the faith.

Farther and farther west he pushed. Away out in Albion, Wisconsin, he found a Brother Perry, who had made arrangements for a conference of believers to meet in the church of the Seventh Day Baptists. They had also fixed up a place for worship in a grove near the meeting house. Elder Bates here preached to over four hundred people. Some had come five, thirty, and even seventy miles on foot and in wagons to hear the truth presented.

The following month he wrote from Milan, Ohio, where with Brother Dodge, a convert from Jackson, he held meetings. Together they visited many places in the northern part of the state. They met some violent opposers of the message, but also found some who "were famishing for the present truth," as Bates reported.

In November he once more visited the towns and villages in Massachusetts, Vermont, and New York. His last place of call was Buck's Bridge, in New York, where a conference was held in the house of John Byington. This man had been a preacher for the Wesleyan Methodists, but after carefully examining the truth, he and his family decided to stand for the Sabbath. Ten years later this same John Byington was elected the first president of the newly formed General Conference.

Early in January Elder Bates returned to Fairhaven after an absence of three months and happily found his family well. His visit with them was brief, for the following month he was off again, holding meetings in many scattered towns in Massachusetts. Coming to Athol, he was told of an Adventist brother who had been desperately ill and was given only ten days in which to live. Elder Bates was taken to his home, where he found him weak in body, but with a clear mind. Here again Elder Bates presented the third angel's message in his usual clear way, and the man indicated his full acceptance. Elder Bates then anointed him and prayed for his recovery. When the prayer was finished, the man arose, dressed, and walked out of the sickroom, praising the Lord for what He had done.

Many times he met with dangerous fanaticism in the ranks of professed Sabbathkeepers. At a meeting at Ellenwoods he presented the subject of the sanctuary and its cleansing. Afterward some of the leading members of the congregation began shouting, praying aloud, and exhorting; they stamped and pounded the floor with their chairs. They said they were trying to convert Elder Bates to see that the church was the true sanctuary and that it must be cleansed.

Elder Bates calmly objected to their views, presenting strong arguments from the Bible to show they were wrong. One of the leaders then crossed the room, seized Bates by the shoulders, and shook him most violently.

'Why do you attack me like this?" asked Elder Bates.

"Ah, it is not I that is attacking you," shouted the man; "it is the Spirit trying to shake your errors out of you."

"I warn you, brethren," replied the minister, "that actions of this kind will avail you nothing. You must learn to worship God with reverence and holy fear." Then he left them and went on his way.

Before the year was over Elder Bates was writing reports from Olena, Ohio; Jackson, Michigan; and Sullivan, Indiana. In spite of the "cold and stony" hearts which he often encountered, there was never a word of discouragement in any of his reports.

The end of November found him once more resting with his family and brethren in Fairhaven, having been absent for six months. Did he remain here through the winter? Not Elder Bates! Within a month he was writing from Jackson, Michigan, three days after Christmas. Somehow that church, the first fruits of his labors in the West, was particularly dear to the heart of Elder Bates.

From here he felt impressed to visit Rochester, New York, to confer with the workers there. Never was a visit more timely. The Whites had been passing through a time of great trial. Elder White's own brother, Nathaniel, had recently died of tuberculosis. He himself had been seriously ill, and his wife feared that he would not live long. Money was scarce with which to carry on the work, and at times there was little in the house to eat.

"Elder Bates, we are most happy to see you!" exclaimed Elder White, clasping the rough hand of the pioneer. "You shall spend the Sabbath and first day with us."

Uriah and Annie Smith, hearing the voice of Joseph Bates, left their work and joined Elder White in welcoming their spiritual father.

"How are my children in the Lord?" asked Bates with a warm smile, extending his hand to them.

The visit of Elder Bates brought fresh courage and confidence to the tired workers at the office. Their hearts thrilled as he related how little companies were springing up in towns and villages. The papers they were sending out so

Elder Bates-Christian gentleman and Advent crusader.

faithfully, he assured them, were doing a mighty work. *The Review and Herald* was bringing a wonderful spirit of unity into the ranks of Sabbathkeepers. They could now rest assured that God was blessing the publications.

Thus Elder Bates continued his work, year in and year out, summer and winter, like the Apostle Paul—poor, yet making many rich; sorrowful, yet always rejoicing. To him no effort was ever too great if it would result in bringing yet more souls into what he referred to as "the blessed hope."

Chapter Twenty-Four

Sunset

NEAR the close of 1855 Elder and Mrs. White, with the group of faithful workers who had been helping in the publishing work in Rochester, moved to Battle Creek, Michigan. This was to be the headquarters of our work for nearly half a century. Elder Bates was happy to learn that the money used to buy land and erect a building for *the Review and Herald* publishing work was given by four faithful members of his beloved church in Jackson, one of whom had sold his farm to raise the necessary funds. The former pull for him to move to Michigan was now stronger than ever. It was no great surprise to Mrs. Bates when her husband again spoke of the subject.

"Well, Prudy," Elder Bates remarked one day in 1858, "I have decided to move to Michigan."

"I have been rather expecting it, Joseph, although I cannot say I am too happy over the move. I have lived for nearly forty years in this vicinity, and all of my friends are here in Fairhaven. However, where you go, I shall go." Mrs. Bates laid her hand lovingly on the arm of her husband.

"Shall we be settling in Battle Creek?" she asked.

"No, I am not planning to go to that center. Enough ministers are there now to care for the needs of the community. I feel strongly drawn to a farming community I once visited known as Monterey, lying between Battle Creek and Lake Michigan."

A few weeks later Joseph Bates and his wife moved to their new home in the West, where they were to live for the next thirteen years.

This move did not mean that Elder Bates was retiring or slowing down in his missionary activities. He felt a burden to see young men trained for the kind of work he had been doing. He often invited first one young man, then another, to accompany him on his preaching trips, giving them an opportunity to speak in public, then giving them fatherly counsel and kindly criticism. John Corliss, who later became one of the leading ministers, thus received valuable experience working with Elder Bates. The simple manner in which the older minister looked to God for guidance in all the affairs of life, talking to Him with quiet earnestness and familiar confidence, deeply impressed young Corliss. Years later he confessed that after hearing Bates in prayer, he had felt as did the disciples who requested the Master to teach them to pray.

Elder Bates sometimes seemed to have prophetic vision. At a meeting held in Jackson a young man, little more than a boy, heard and confessed the truth. When mentioning his name a few days later, Brother Bates said that the young man would sometime carry the message with success. This youth was I. D. Van Horn, one of the early efficient workers in the cause.

One afternoon John Corliss was staying with Elder Bates when a man came requesting the now elderly minister to conduct a series of Bible studies in a nearby community. Elder Bates startled the visitor by saying abruptly, "I am too old to go. Here is a young man who will help you," pointing to John Corliss.

Elder Bates then laid his hand gently on John's head and said, "Now prime yourself, young man, and get ready." There was nothing for Corliss to do but go and learn by experience how to do it himself.

Those were tremendous years in the Advent Movement. Joseph Bates shared in all the developments of the growing church. In 1860 he took part in a meeting when the name "Seventh-day Adventist" was chosen to signify the remnant church. The following year he presided at a meeting when the Michigan Conference was organized, the first of many. He was chosen as the first president of this conference. Two years later he was one of the delegates from the state of Michigan to attend the meeting in Battle Creek when the General Conference was organized. Although he might have been one of the officers of the General Conference, he expressed the feeling that his work lay along other lines. In 1868, he, his wife, and three hundred other believers attended our first camp meeting, which was held in a maple forest at Wright, Michigan. There he was one of a number of ministers who bore messages to the campers.

Through the years that remained to him, the zeal of Joseph Bates never flagged. Seldom was he at home for more than a week or a fortnight at a time. Many times he was turned away from homes to which he sought entrance, but he never became discouraged, never showed anything but a Christlike spirit to those who rejected him and his message. We have no records enabling us to know the number of his converts during the years of his ministry, but we can be certain that his crown in heaven will glitter with stars.

In 1865 Elder Bates returned from a trip among the churches and found a letter from an eastern shipping company. The owner informed him with deep regret that the vessel on which Joseph, their only surviving son had sailed, was now long overdue and must be given up as lost with all hands. This came as a severe blow to the aged parents, who turned to the Lord in their hour of bereavement and found comfort in His promises.

Many requests came to Elder Bates to write the record of his experiences, first about his years at sea, and then about his entrance into the first Advent movement. Ten years previously, in response to similar requests, he had prepared a series of over fifty articles which had run through *The Youth's Instructor* over a period of three years. In the sunset years of his life, he now assembled these articles and prepared them for publication in book form. His *Life of Joseph Bates* was dispatched from Monterey to the publishers in May, 1868.

When the Lord sent light to His people on the subject of health reform through His servant, Mrs. E. G. White, Joseph Bates truly rejoiced. For more than thirty years he had made steady progress in the work of reforming his own life, discarding first alcoholic drinks, then tobacco, tea, coffee, flesh meats, rich pastries, cakes, pies, spices, etc. Anything which he felt was harmful to his body he discarded with iron resolution.

Elder Bates was not a man who went around preaching and urging others to imitate him in this aspect of life, but when he was asked to give a reason for his health principles, he never hesitated. Once when questioned as to why he no longer ate flesh meats, he quietly replied, "I have eaten my share of them."

One day another question was put to him. "Elder Bates, we hear you don't drink tea or coffee."

He replied, "That's true! They are poison. Some thirty-five years ago I was using both tea and coffee. After retiring from a tea party at midnight, my bed companion said, 'What is the matter? Can't you lie quietly and sleep?' 'Sleep! No!' I replied. 'Why not?' was the next question. 'Oh, I wish Mrs. Bunker's tea had stayed in the East Indies. It's poison!' Here I bade farewell to tea and coffee. After a while my wife joined me, and we have discarded them from our table and dwelling."

While he could be very tolerant of the habits of others, he was extremely strict with himself. No amount of pleading could get him to transgress the rules he had laid down for keeping his body healthy. One Fourth of July he attended a picnic with a church in Vassar, Michigan, where he spoke to the adults and their children in a barn and was then invited to share their picnic dinner. The tables were laden with tempting delicacies and there was even swine's flesh, as this was prior to the time when instruction had come on that subject. When he was invited to return thanks for the food and ask God's blessing on it, he was careful to request a blessing on all the *clean, nutritious, wholesome, lawful* food. A number of people present smiled, but the lesson was not lost.

The wonderful health which Joseph Bates enjoyed was sometimes a mystery to his ministerial brethren. It was always their envy. The leaders of the cause in those early days—White, Smith, Loughborough, Waggoner, Andrews, and others—all suffered more or less from various physical afflictions, but not Bates. Year in and year out he continued, working his body through the heat of summer and the chilling frosts of winter with never a complaint of aches or pains. The wonderful point is that never once, so far as we can discover, did he reprove his brethren for their dietary habits or suggest to them that they might enjoy health like his if they would be willing to follow his health practices.

One day early in August, 1870, Elder Bates, while traveling in northern Michigan, received a letter from his "beloved companion Prudy," as he so frequently called her. In it she expressed the earnest longing "to have my mind free from care and so many household duties that I may more exclusively give my mind and time to the all-important subject of getting just right before the Lord." Perhaps it was premonition arising from the serious tone of the letter which drew the steps of the now aged evangelist once more toward his home in Monterey. On the seventeenth of the month she was taken with a fever which continued intermittently for ten days. Her husband watched tenderly by her bedside, but it was evident that she was sinking, and he would shortly be left to continue life alone.

On Sabbath afternoon a service was being held in the Monterey church. The elders gathered and, with the husband and father, bowed around the bedside of Prudence Bates and earnestly prayed that God's will might be done. Just as the hour for meeting arrived, Prudy opened her eyes to see her husband standing near, torn between his desire to attend the meeting and what he felt to be his duty to remain by her side. Having lived with her Joseph for fifty-two years, she knew him very well and with a feeble wave of her hand bade him, "Go to meeting." On his return he found her sinking fast, and ere the sun had set she closed her eyes and fell asleep.

From this time on we catch only fleeting glimpses of Elder Bates. Although, like Moses, his eye was not dimmed nor his natural force abated, he took meekly the advice of his brethren and restricted his activities. After the death of his wife his daughter came to live with him and keep his home.

In the spring of 1871 he was in Battle Creek and attended a health reform rally called to revive interest in that important subject. As part of the program, various individuals rose and told what the health message had done for them, both spiritually and physically. Suddenly someone called out: "Where is Elder Bates? We must hear Elder Bates on this subject."

Elder Bates was modestly sitting in the rear of the congregation. In response to this request, he walked down the aisle, and those who saw him said afterwards that he tripped along as nimbly as a boy and stood as straight as a marble shaft.

On the platform he told in a clear, ringing voice the story of how through the years he had dropped one bad habit after another until he had reached the point of total abstinence from everything harmful. In closing he said he was entirely free from aches and pains and faced the gladdening and cheering prospect that if he continued on in the way he had chosen, he would stand without fault before the throne of God.

The audience was so electrified by the old man's eloquence that for a few moments only deep "Amens" could be heard from all parts of the congregation. He was at that time in his seventy-ninth year.

His last letter, written less than six weeks before his death, was to Sister White in response to one he had received from her expressing fears that he was not eating enough.

"God bless you, Sister White," he wrote, "for your favor of yesterday, the twelfth. You say I must have good nutritious food." He then proceeded to list the various kinds of foodstuffs he had in his house and the amount of each, showing that he was starving neither himself nor his daughter.

"Starving, with more than enough to eat?" he concluded. "I am now well supplied with good nutritious food. If there is any lack, I have some good, faithful brethren who seem to be waiting to serve me."

"I am your brother, now on retired pay, in Monterey, Michigan." This letter was dated February 14, 1872.

Shortly after, he was attacked by a particularly malignant type of erysipelas which caused his death on March 19 in the Battle Creek Sanitarium. They carried him back to Monterey and laid him to rest by the side of his faithful, loving companion. The Advent people mourned deeply, for there was scarcely a church east or west, north or south, in which his converts were not found or which had not been uplifted by his loving, hopeful messages.

When his last will and testament was opened shortly after his death, it was found that he had left his property to his wife, should he precede her. In the event of his outliving her, his home and farm were to be sold and the entire proceeds given to the Seventh-day Adventist Publishing Association of Battle Creek. This was done.

To the very end his life was consistent with the principle he had adopted when he first became a Christian: "All that I am, all that I have, belongs to God."

Bibliography

Books

Bates, Joseph, *The Autobiography of Elder Joseph Bates*, James White, ed. Battle Creek, Michigan, The Seventh-day Adventist Publishing Association, 1877.

Loughborough, J. N., *Rise and Progress of Seventh-day Adventists*. General Conference Association of Seventh-day Adventists (Battle Creek, Michigan, 1892), pp. 109-113, 125-131.

Robinson, D. E., *The Story of Our Health Message*, Southern Publishing Association (Nashville, Tennessee, 1943), pp. 45-52.

Spalding, A. W., *Footprints of the Pioneers*, Review and Herald Publishing Association (Washington, D.C., 1947), pp. 34-48, 139-146, 157-169.

Spalding, A. W., *Captains of the Host*, Review and Herald Publishing Association (Washington, D.C., 1949), pp. 29-43, 171-187, 194-196, 223-232.

White, Mrs. Ellen G., *Life Sketches of Ellen G. White*, compiled from original sources, Pacific Press Publishing Association (Mountain View, California, 1915), pp. 95, 96, 110-115.

Periodicals

Bates, Joseph, Letters to *The Advent Review and Sabbath Herald*.

    Vol. II, No.1 (August 5, 1851), p. 6.

    Vol. II, No. 10 (January 13, 1852), p. 80.

    Vol. III, No.1 (May 6, 1852), pp. 6, 7.

    Vol. III, No.5 (July 8, 1852), p. 40.

    Vol. III, No.6 (July 22, 1852), p. 47.

    Vol. III, No.9 (September 2, 1852), p. 69.

    Vol. III, No. 17 (January 6, 1853), p. 135.

    Vol. III, No. 19 (February 3, 1853), p. 151.

    Vol. III, No. 23 (March 31, 1853), pp. 182, 183.

Corliss, J. O., "Joseph Bates as I Knew Him." *The Advent Review and Sabbath Herald*, Vol. 100 (August 16, 1923), pp. 7, 8.

Loughborough, J. N., "Second Advent Experience," No. 3. *The Advent Review and Sabbath Herald*, Vol. 100 (June 21, 1923), pp. 5,6.

Loughborough, J. N., "Second Advent Experience," No.7. *The Advent Review and Sabbath Herald*, Vol. 100 (July 26, 1923), p. 5.

We invite you to view the complete
selection of titles we publish at:

www.TEACHServices.com

Scan with your mobile
device to go directly
to our website.

Please write or email us your praises, reactions,
or thoughts about this or any other book we publish at:

TEACH Services, Inc.
P U B L I S H I N G
www.TEACHServices.com

P.O. Box 954
Ringgold, GA 30736

info@TEACHServices.com

TEACH Services, Inc., titles may be purchased in bulk for
educational, business, fund-raising, or sales promotional use.
For information, please e-mail:

BulkSales@TEACHServices.com

Finally, if you are interested in seeing
your own book in print, please contact us at

publishing@TEACHServices.com

We would be happy to review your manuscript for free.